Time In,
Time Out

SUPER 7 DAYS   EOM

-4 EOM +3

FAD BNC — MID/MOS

3RD FRIDAY SHORTING OPTION OPTION
EXPIRATION DATES

Time In,
Time Out

Outsmart the Market Using
Calendar Investment Strategies

Brooke Thackray, MBA, CIM, CFP
Bruce Lindsay, CFP

MEDIA

Published in 2000 by: **Upwave Media Inc.**

1275 Hollyfield Crescent
Oakville, Ontario
Canada
L6H 2J5
Bus: (905) 844-9955
Fax: (905) 844-2456

10 Winners Circle
Penfield, NY
14526

www.upwave.com

Distributed by: Hushion House Publishing Limited
36 Northline Road
Toronto, Ontario, Canada
M4B 3E2
Telephone: (416) 285-6100

Library of Congress Control Number: 00-133728

Canadian Cataloguing-in-Publication Data

ISBN 1-890412-937

Cover design: Robert MacDonald

NOTE: *Time In, Time Out* contains the opinions and the findings of its authors. It is sold understanding that the authors and publisher are not engaged in rendering legal, accounting, investment or other professional services. If the reader requires further financial or other assistance, a professional CFP practitioner or licensed investment advisor should be consulted. Every effort has been made to ensure completeness and accuracy of the information herein. The authors and publisher assume no responsibility for any errors, omissions or inconsistencies.

Printed and bound in Canada by Webcom Ltd.

00 09 9 8 7 6 5 4 3 2

To our spouses, Jane Steer-Thackray

and Brenda Lindsay, for their love,

understanding and help during this

project.

CONTENTS

Acknowledgments

The authors wish to thank the many people who have provided assistance and inspiration throughout the course of preparing this book. In particular:

Richard Au and Luke Thackray, for creating software for the numerical analysis.

Anthony Cacciacarro, for tackling the tough job of editing and layout of the book.

Robert McDonald, for crafting the cover and lending his artistic talents in general.

Carolina Saffioti, for giving us insight into all matters related to production of the project.

Jane Thackray, for additional editorial comments.

Finally, loving thanks to our families for their patience and encouragement.

Disclaimer

This book contains performance data and related statements based on historic data culled from a variety of sources. While great care was taken to ensure accuracy, no warranty is given that actual results were achieved by anyone to the same extent shown. Moreover, past performance of stocks, funds, or stock indices are no indication of future performance. Investors should request a prospectus and seek professional guidance before investing in any of the specific products mentioned.

The example portfolio information is for illustration only and prospective purchasers of mentioned securities should consult with their registered advisors before considering implementation. The authors are no longer active in the investment industry as registered representatives, so any comments made regarding investment products are not done as specific investment recommendations, rather as general information for the public.

The authors currently hold the Certified Financial Planner™ (CFP™) designation awarded in Canada by Financial Planners Standards Council to individuals who meet its certification requirements. As such they encourage readers to consult with a professional CFP practitioner regarding issues of asset mix and appropriateness of various investments for their personal circumstances, before implementation of any ideas contained herein.

Introduction

As stock brokers we were taught that the stock market was totally random. Nothing is further from the truth. All that you need to beat the market is a calendar.

Over the years, we came to notice that the market seemed to move in cycles, having similar high and low points on both a monthly and yearly basis. We wanted to unravel the mystery of the cyclical action in the market and reveal common patterns. We knew from experience that uncovering them could be a tremendous benefit to all investors.

At night and on weekends, we pored over historical market data and charts, searching for any possible repetitive patterns. Data that dated back to 1953 was collected and calendar models were developed. As we put the numbers together, it was astounding to see the success of our various forms of calendar investment strategies as they easily and consistently beat the Dow Jones Industrial Average.

With these investment strategies in mind, we have developed a simple system to beat the market by relying on predetermined calendar dates. There is a huge opportunity for both the long-term and short-term investor to substantially increase their returns using our efficient calendar system. The long-term investor need only focus on two days a year: one buy date and one sell date to dramatically beat the Dow. The short-term trader is given the best intervals throughout the calendar year for making quick profits.

Not only did we develop a system that beats the market, but it also offers investors unique advantages not present in other systems. Our plan allows you to invest with less risk and less stress. It also allows you to take a break from the market every year so that you can have that much-needed vacation. As advisors, we found that most investors worry about their investments far too much (even if they proclaim that they do not). The truth is that the more investments decline, the more investors worry and begin to question why they ever bother to invest in the market at all. *Time In Time Out* provides the necessary relief with its integral "Time Out" period when there is no exposure to the market at all.

We know that there will be many skeptics of our system because we are going against the status quo of "buy, hold, and close your eyes". We are also going against the mistaken belief that you need to use sophisticated market timing models, economic indicators, or technical analysis to make an educated investment. These issues do not concern us since we know that our system works, which in the final analysis is all that really matters. Sometimes the financial industry is slow to adopt new ideas, especially if they are uncomplicated or unprofitable for them.

As investors become more and more frustrated with waiting out the declines in the market or by incorrectly buying high and selling low, the industry will start to see the merits of our system. Perhaps at that point, they will start to develop products that incorporate the fundamental principles of *Time In Time Out* for the general public. Until then, only you as the *individual investor* can select both the time to profit from market advances, and the time to protect your capital from market declines. Your task will be made easier with the knowledge gained from this book.

Over the last two years, we have witnessed a number of rational clients become obsessed with the stock market. They transformed from conservative buy and hold or mutual fund investors, to stock-pickers, to tech stock speculators, and finally to market timers. A few even became day traders! All of this was in the hope of outperforming the market, friends, family, co-workers, or even that brother-in-law who was lucky enough to buy a hot stock three years ago and make a million dollars. Our better judgement tells us that there is something dangerously wrong with this situation. When people abandon their long-standing beliefs and objectives to pursue a more exciting and ultimately riskier investor profile, they jeopardize their financial future.

For this reason, we were motivated to write this book and help anyone interested in succeeding with the stock market. We wanted to eliminate most of the risk and heartache that investors experience when using other methods of investing.

Time In Time Out is a system that relies on calendar trends to produce above average returns and give you time off from the markets. Whether you make your own decisions or work with an advisor, use an active trading strategy or prefer a more passive approach, you will find something of value in the calendar trends detailed herein. It is our sincerest hope that you find the system as easy and profitable to use as we have, and benefit personally and financially.

Brooke Thackray, Bruce Lindsay

Part 1

Introduction to *Time In Time Out*

This part of the book serves as an introduction, explaining what *Time In, Time Out* is and how it was developed. There are five chapters in this part, and highlights from each are as follows:

- **A New Approach to Investing:** introduces the calendar investing system, its origins, and provides statistics to show the performance.
- **Why The Annual Cycle Works:** illustrates factors behind the success of the system.
- **Who Can Use *Time In, Time Out*:** includes a variety of scenarios and examples illustrating the type of people that can use this system.
- **Calendar Investing: Who Will Tell You About It?:** explains why you may not have heard about calendar investing from the financial industry.
- **Calendar Investing Criticisms—No Longer Valid:** debunks previous criticisms of calendar investing.
- **Succeeding Where Traditional Methods Fail:** shows how *Time In, Time Out* compares with the traditional investment strategies.

A New Approach to Investing

Are you looking for a way to make more money in the stock market? Are you a short-term or long-term investor looking to increase your returns? Are you a novice investor that would like to enter the stock market with a safe investment plan? Do you want above average returns with less risk than the overall stock market? Are you looking for a system that is easy to use and does not require much time?

We have devised a system called *Time In Time Out* that allows you to answer "yes" to all of the above questions. It does not matter if you are a professional trader or a novice; using our system, you will be able to beat the market. You do not have to follow any complicated trading strategies, interpret any data, draw charts or wait for signals. All that you need to beat the market is a calendar.

What is Calendar Investing?

"Calendar investing" is a term that we have coined. It describes the method of making buy and sell decisions based upon when the market has typically risen or fallen. It can very loosely be referred to as a form of seasonal investment timing. In the past, several people have advocated using a form of seasonal timing, but the suggested methods were not as thorough as *Time In Time Out*. We wanted to pick up where others left off, and develop a full-fledged system with firm entry and exit calendar dates that anyone can use repetitively and confidently.

Historically, markets have tended to rise and fall at the same time of the month or year. By knowing the calendar trends of the market, you can beat it, and with less risk. Our system has done this consistently over a number of decades. Whether you are a long-term or short-term investor, this book will tell you all the dates that you need to know to increase your profits.

Time In Time Out—A Straightforward System

Most other investment systems in use are cumbersome and difficult. They require investors to devote a lot of time following the markets, interpreting graphs and performing numerical calculations. Very often, investors becomes frustrated and confused. Although investors may try these types of systems, they typically do not stay with them very long.

Time In Time Out is different. At any point during the year, you can sit down and circle your buy and sell dates on a calendar for the entire year. All of these dates are predetermined based upon historical market trends.

Throughout all of the cycles that we detail in this book, **Time In** refers to the period when you are invested in the market. **Time Out** refers to the period when you are **not** invested in the market.

Because *Time In Time Out* is so easy to use, it is a life-long system. Investments do not need to dominate your life as you do not have to concern yourself with the valuation or direction of the market at any time. *Time In Time Out* can achieve above average returns with little or no time spent managing your portfolio because our system puts probability on your side. All of these elements make *Time In Time Out* a straightforward system.

Easy to Use Annual Cycle (for Long-Term Investors)

The Annual Cycle is discussed in Part One and Part Two.

To beat the market, the Annual Cycle is structured to put you into the market for the time of the year that the market typically rises, and take you out when the market typically declines. It relies on only two transactions per year: one buy and one sell. The buy date is the same date every year and the sell date is the same date every year. Figure 1.1 shows how easy this strategy is to use.

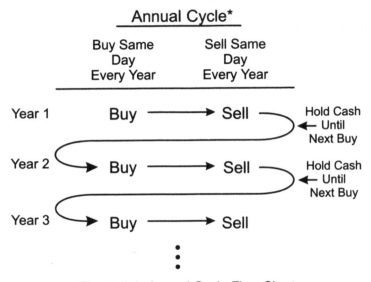

Figure 1.1: Annual Cycle Flow Chart

*Later in the book we show the benefits of using this system over different years and decades. We also include different scenarios of interest being earned when you are not invested in the market, and dividends being paid when you are in the market.

Easy To Use Hot Cycles (for Short-Term Investors)

The Hot Cycles are discussed in Part Three of the book.

Our Hot Cycles are classified as either monthly or extended-short cycles. The monthly cycles take advantage of the trends that reoccur every month. There are two extended-short cycles that last for 55 days and 100 days, and occur once a year.

The Super Seven is a good example of how easy the monthly cycles are to use. It takes advantage of the seven days around month end that tend to significantly outperform the daily market average. All that you have to do is buy four trading days before the end of the month and sell three trading days into the next month. This strategy can be used repetitively almost every month.

Time In Time Out Beats The Market

Both the Annual Cycle and the Hot Cycles outperformed the market significantly. One of the major criteria that we used when designing these cycles was that the average investor would be able to beat the market. They should be able to look at any one of our cycles and feel confident that the dates given to buy and sell produce above average returns.

The Annual Cycle Crushes a Buy and Hold Strategy

The Annual Cycle has worked over the short-term and long-term, and across the major North American markets. The following tables show how our Annual Cycle performed against some of the major market indices from 1998 to 1999. For this comparison and all other comparisons with the Annual Cycle, the indices are invested on a buy and hold basis. The Annual Cycle enters and exits the market on predetermined dates each year.

The TSE300 is the Toronto stock exchange and is included for our Canadian readers. This index tends to move with the American markets as the economies are so closely linked, and many of the large cap stocks on the TSE300 are inter-listed on the New York stock exchange.

Please note that the abbreviations *TITO* and *TT* refer to the *Time In Time Out* system for the following tables, and throughout the remainder of this book.

Table 1.1: Comparison of the Dow Jones Index and TITO

Year	Dow	*TITO*	Difference	*TITO* Improvement
1998	15.30%	28.70%	+13.4%	87.6%
1999	24.7%	36.9%	+12.2%	49.4%

Table 1.2: Comparison of S&P500 Index and TITO

Year	S&P500	*TITO*	Difference	*TITO* Improvement
1998	26.66%	43.92%	+17.26%	64.7%
1999	19.63%	32.46%	+12.83%	65.3%

Table 1.3: Comparison of the Nasdaq Index and TITO

Year	Nasdaq	*TITO*	Difference	*TITO* Improvement
1998	39.63	65.10	+25.47%	64.3%
1999	85.59	89.49	+3.9%	4.5%

Table 1.4: Comparison of TSE300 and TITO

Year	TSE300	*TITO*	Difference	*TITO* Improvement
1998	-3.36	17.99	+21.35%	*
1999	28.35	32.67	+4.32%	15.2%

NOTE: *TITO* Improvement is % premium of the index return
* = percentage calculation unavailable due to negative buy and hold performance

The results for 1998 and 1999 are excellent. We did not just beat the market by a little, we beat it by a lot. There are very few mutual funds that have achieved the same level of performance as our system. Also, despite the number of investors making a lot of money during this time period, very few can claim that they did as well as our system.

The four major markets have been included in this example to show you that our system is not just limited to the Dow Jones index. In all cases the Annual Cycle beat the index. Although we beat the Nasdaq in 1999, it was our least advantageous result. We were still able to achieve **89.49%**, or an extra 3.9% compared with the buy and hold strategy.

The excellent results of the Annual Cycle are not just limited to the last two years. Our system has performed very well over all timeframes. Figure 1.2 shows the long-term results of a $100,000 initial investment, using the Annual Cycle against the major North American market indices.

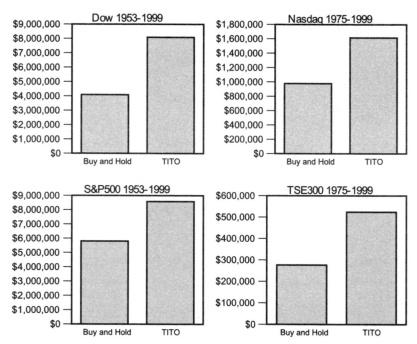

Figure 1.2: Annual Cycle Returns for Major North American Indices

The results that the Annual Cycle achieved are absolutely incredible. To put them into perspective, it must be remembered that only 11% of the mutual fund managers have beaten the index over the last ten years, and an even smaller percentage of managers (4%) beat the market on a fifteen year basis (McLean 2). To the best of our knowledge, there are no fund managers that have beaten the market for the entire 1953 to 1999 period.

We performed significantly better than a buy and hold strategy for all of the North American indices. Investing $100,000 in the Dow in 1953 with our system, produced $8.1 million dollars in 1999. This resulted in **198% of the Dow return**; a "Doubling the Dow" strategy.

The Hot Cycle Days Beat the Market

For a short-term investor, every advantage counts. Our strategies can give you a distinct edge over the market by providing you with the best possible days to make your investments. These days produce significantly better returns when compared with market daily average.

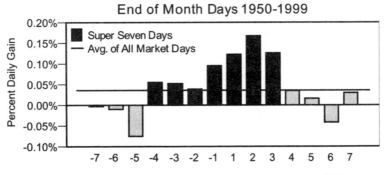

Figure 1.3: End of Month Trading Days, 1950 to 1999

Our Super Seven strategy has produced incredible results over the last fifty years. In Figure 1.3, the Super Seven days (the last four days of the month and the first three of the next month) have daily returns that are significantly above the average daily market return. The Super Seven days have produced results that are over two and a half times better than the market average. Knowing that these days are so much better allows you to invest with greater confidence.

If you had used the Super Seven strategy from 1950 to 1999, you would have made 79% of the Dow total return. The Dow total return was calculated by entering the market on January 1st, 1950 and exiting on December 31st, 1999. The Super Seven return was calculated by investing once a month for seven days, for all of the months between 1950 and 1999. When you consider that our strategy exposes you to the market for one-third of the time compared with a buy and hold strategy, achieving 79% of the total return is an excellent result.

Peace of Mind for the Long-Term Investor

One of the intangible benefits that cannot be measured is the peace of mind that you can get by being out of the markets during volatile times when the market is declining. Volatility is a measurement of how much prices are changing or fluctuating. If there are big price changes in the market, volatility is high. If the market is fairly flat or price changes are small, volatility is low.

As brokers, we used to receive a lot of calls from our clients when the markets were volatile and prices were falling. Most investors became very concerned in this situation. They began to think about how much money they could lose if the large price drop continued. Even when the net result of the high volatility did not mean much to the overall price movement, investors were uneasy. They much preferred to see steady gains in a fairly calm market.

Figure 1.4 shows that the Annual Cycle helps provide peace of mind to investors by pulling them out of the market during the increasingly volatile time from August to October.

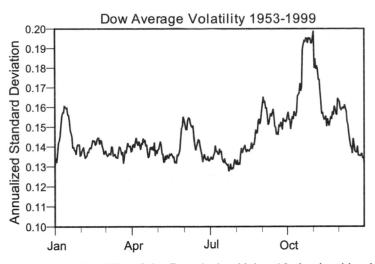

Figure 1.4: Volatility of the Dow Index Using 10-day Lookback

As you can see from this graph, since 1953, volatility has been relatively calm from the beginning of the year through to the spring or summer months. Volatility then surges in August through to October, during the Time Out period. Finally, it returns to normal levels and drops to a lower level in the late fall.

A Vacation for both the Long-Term and Short-Term Investor

Many people have become obsessed with investment information during the great bull market of the last few years. They feel they must be constantly updated with what is going on in the markets and their own investments. To meet the increasing appetite for information there has been a proliferation of financial websites, such as Bloomberg, Yahoo Finance, Big Charts, and The Street.com. The media has also complied with this request with more in-depth, and at times, continuous coverage of financial news such as the FMOC meetings. The investing public has demonstrated a huge appetite for this type of coverage. It is not uncommon to see patrons of a sports bar checking their stock prices on a television hanging overhead.

Investors now live in a world where they have more information than ever, yet increasingly they feel out of control unless they are glued to a television or a computer. They constantly wonder how they are going to be effected by a fast-breaking news story or if they are going to be able to act soon enough to stem a major loss. Currently the market has extended trading hours, and there is a promise of a twenty-four hour global market in the near future. It will soon be possible to make or lose money while you are sleeping.

Time In Time Out gives you the time away from the markets that you need, enabling you to enjoy the other things in life. Being out of the market when it typically declines, reduces your stress level and allows you to enjoy life. It is like having a vacation. Since you do not have any money at risk, you will not feel the need to "just check" the status of your investments with your broker, or find the nearest computer terminal to check your online trading account. Instead, you can sit back and enjoy the benefits of a well-deserved vacation.

Reviewing the merits of *Time In Time Out*, it:
- Is a new system, unlike any other
- Does not rely on guesswork
- Has outperformed the indices, short and long-term
- Works for all major North American market indices
- Has only two transactions per year for the Annual Cycle
- Protects your capital during declines
- Gives you peace of mind
- Gives you a break from the market.

Why The Annual Cycle Works

There has been much debate as to why the market generally rises and falls at the same time year after year. Many people have speculated on the rationale for the seasonal trends, but no one can be certain as to why the market behaves the way it does. In the first part of this chapter, we will discuss the possible reasons why the market exhibits seasonality. Even if you disagree with our explanations of why the trends exist, the results show that using the Annual Cycle is still going to make you more money than a buy and hold strategy. In the second part of this chapter, we will show how effectively the Annual Cycle has avoided the market losses that can severely damage a portfolio.

Seasonal Factors

The stock market is directed in part by the amount of money that flows into it. If investors are putting new money in, it tends to rise: if investors are taking money out, it tends to decline. Examining all the factors that affect seasonal money flow helps to establish and understand the times when the market is most likely to change direction. Unfortunately, there are no available statistics for these factors, hence, they are presented as observations from our experience in the industry.

New Money in the Market

Employees, small-company owners and shareholders tend to receive bonuses and dividends toward the end of the calendar year. The money is often in the form of a lump sum, over and above what is needed for normal living expenses, and a portion of this money is directed into the stock market, pushing up its value.

Retirement Savings Boosting the Market

Contributions to non-taxable accounts such as 401(k)'s in the United States and RRSP's in Canada, increase money flow into the market. In recent years, most individuals are electing to have a larger portion of their accounts in equities, creating more demand for stocks. Investors tend to contribute to their registered accounts late in the year or early in the next year. Since the possibility of a time delay for investment exists, the money flowing into the market causes stock prices to rise from November right through to May.

The Fall Fear Factor

Another cause for seasonal trends comes in the form of individual psychology. The way people think and feel play an important role in making decisions. The fall is historically a bad time for the stock market, punctuated by periods of pessimism and crashes. For example, in the past dozen years the fall period has been influenced by sour memories of the 1987 crash. Investors simply stayed out of the market altogether during September and October. This served to exacerbate any slight weakness that did exist, making August, September and October three of the worst months for the market.

Each year when the end of October arrives, investors regain their confidence and start putting money back into the market. They feel comfortable once they escape the decline for another year. As you will see later in this book, the months immediately following this uncertain fall period are one of the best times to be in the market.

Investor Focus Factor

The market has historically experienced lower trading volume with lower prices during the summer and fall. Many people believe that this is a result of investors losing focus in the markets during the summer months while vacationing. At this time they are more focused on enjoying themselves and spending money, rather than on their investments.

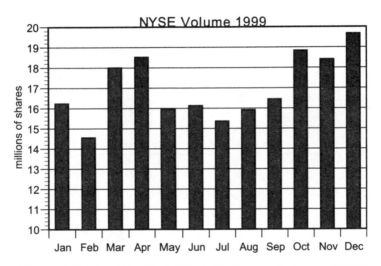

Figure 2.5: The New York Stock Exchange Volume of 1999

The above graph illustrates the seasonal tendency of trading volumes declining during the summer months. This period is when the Time In Time Out system signals you to be out of the market. While this data covers only 1999, it is representative of the general trend.

Cash Flow Requirements

From late summer until early fall, investors must contend with many large, annual expenses. Factors such as summer vacation bills, college tuition fees and general back-to-school expenditures create the need for increased cash flow. Many investors sell some of their holdings during this time to pay their bills. The combination of selling investments and a lack of new money flowing into the market, contribute to the general market decline from August to October.

Annual Cycle Avoids Losses

One of the key elements to the success of the *Time In Time Out* system is that it avoids periods of negative performance. An important aspect of making money is reducing your losses, as you have more capital to appreciate during the next market advance. This gives you greater compounding in the long-term. Figure 2.6, an example for illustration purposes, shows how greater results are achieved by avoiding losses.

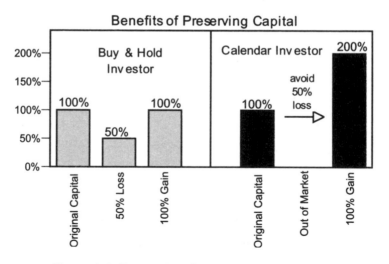

Figure 2.6: Preserving Capital to Increase Profits

Investors using a buy and hold strategy (after suffering a 50% loss), need a 100% gain the following year to return to their original capital position. In comparison, a calendar investor avoiding the 50% decline benefits from the 100% increase and ends up doubling their money.

In Figure 2.7, you can see how much of an impact avoiding losses can have on your total returns over several consecutive periods.

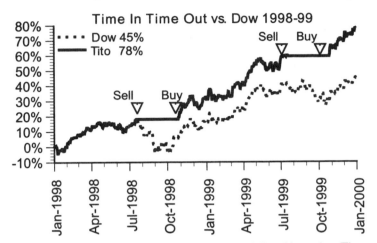

Figure 2.7: Annual Cycle Benefits by Avoiding Negative Times

Key elements of how the Annual Cycle works:

- The up and down patterns that you see on the graph are repetitive throughout history, and not unique to the two years highlighted.
- By selling out of the market in the summer and staying in cash until the fall, downward price movement is avoided and capital is preserved.
- Over these two years the Annual Cycle returned 78%, compared to the Dow's 45%. An extra 33% is achieved by the Annual Cycle.

If you examine the average year over the last ten years, you can see that the same trends exist. In summer time, the market tends to perform negatively before rebounding strongly at the end of October. Figure 2.8 highlights this negative Time Out period that our system avoids. Part Two of the book covers this trend in greater detail.

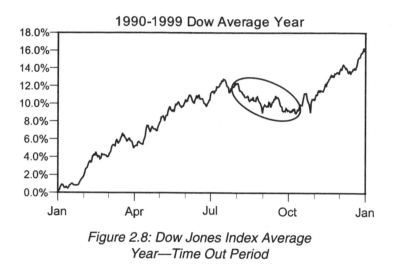

*Figure 2.8: Dow Jones Index Average
Year—Time Out Period*

What impact do losses have on a buy and hold investor?

By not investing during the Time Out period, our system is effective in avoiding losses 51% of the time. If we break *Time In Time Out* into its two components, we can see the impact of the losses during the Time Out cycle. From 1953 to 1999, the following results were produced:

- Buy and hold the Dow = 9.52%
- Time In = 10.97%
- Time Out = -1.18%.

As a buy and hold investor, losing an average of 1.18% per year during the Time Out cycle may not seem like much, but this represents 12% of the Dow yearly gain. On a compounded basis over time, the amount of profit that you would have given up would be substantial.

Figure 2.9 illustrates how the Time Out period has produced a negative return on capital. If you had invested $100,000 in 1953 and re-invested each year during the Time Out period, your original amount would have turned into $52,445. This is a loss of 48%.

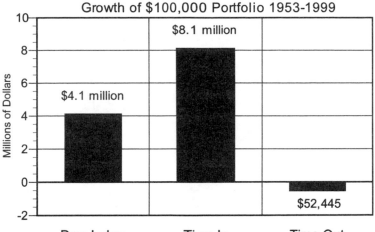

Figure 2.9: Comparing the Dow, Time In and Time Out

Investing only in the Time In period (and avoiding the negative effect of the Time Out period) would have produced a return of $8.1 million, versus the $4.1 million returned for the Dow on a buy and hold basis.

There is no system that is perfect all the time. The key to using the Annual Cycle is to use it over the long-term. There will be years when the buy and hold strategy will produce a small gain during the Time Out period. On the other hand, avoiding the large losses that often occur during the Time Out period will more than make up for any gains you have missed.

In summary, the Annual Cycle works:

- Because of money flow coming into the market as a result of various seasonal factors
- By effectively avoiding losses, giving you a bigger capital base to take advantage of market growth.

Who Can Use *Time In Time Out*

The outstanding feature of *Time In Time Out* is that anyone can use it. It does not matter if you are a novice or experienced investor, or your current style is stockpicking or investing through mutual funds; you can benefit. The same basic principles that help the experienced investor achieve above average returns will help the novice. Although we advocate using index based investments for calendar investing, you can use the system in a complementary fashion with your current investment method.

As certified financial planners, we must inform you of the following items before we can continue:

- Our book is in no way intended to replace professional advice that financial planners can provide. We want to simply help you replace the **guesswork associated with investing the equity portion** of your portfolio.

- All investors should seek the help of a professional CFP practitioner because they can give you a full financial plan that incorporates your individual needs. They will review your asset mix, decide with you the type of implementation strategy to use (buy and hold, stockpicking, *Time In Time Out,* etc.) and they will help you decide what type of investments are appropriate (mutual funds, stocks, etc.).

The Buy And Hold Investor

A buy and hold investor is someone that buys stocks and holds on to them for the long-term, through all of the ups and downs of the market.

There is an opportunity for this type of investor to benefit from our system. Although they may not be interested in buying or selling throughout the year, they may wish to add to their current positions, or sell a holding to raise cash. Calendar investing is a very valuable tool because it gives the investor a roadmap of the low and high times of the market. Adding to a stock position or buying a completely new one at a time when prices are low makes sense, as you get maximum value for your money. The end of the Time Out period in late October is the best time to buy, as stocks are temporarily depressed. On the flip side, selling a holding makes sense when the end of the Time In period has been reached, as prices are high.

The Stockpicking Investor

A stockpicker is an investor that tries to pick individual stocks that have the highest likelihood of going up.

Stockpickers will also find our system useful to help choose the best times to buy and sell. With stockpicking, you can pick the best prospect out of 100 stocks and still watch it go down in a general market decline. Professionals call this the "Good Stock, Bad Timing Syndrome". If you make the decision to buy (or sell) Hewlett Packard, for example, how do you know the best time? If you look at Figure 3.10, you can see that the price fluctuates throughout the year along with the general trend of the market. It makes sense to increase the probability of making money by selecting a low point in the cycle to buy.

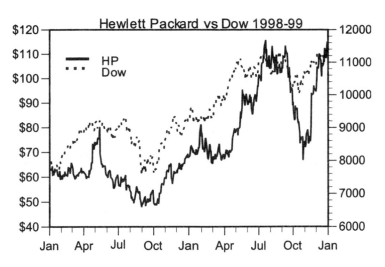

Figure 3.10: Comparison of Hewlett Packard with Dow Index

The Market Timing Investor

The market timing investor is someone who tries to pick the best time to be in and out of the market, and adjusts their investments accordingly.

We believe that our system identifies the best times to buy and sell. If you are interested in using your current timing model, the *Time In Time Out* system can be a valuable resource. You can rely on the identified buy and sell dates to make your market timing decisions.

Risk-adverse Investors

The risk-adverse investor is someone that is very concerned about losing money and is willing to settle for lower returning investments in exchange for greater safety. This group includes, but is not limited to, retirees and travelers. They usually have a large portion of their portfolio invested in fixed income products.

All of these people need to be sure that their capital is safe, and using the Annual Cycle ensures this goal is met by being in cash for the time of the year that the market typically declines. Given the fixed entry and exit points of the system, travelers can arrange in advance to have transactions done for them while they are absent. Using this process, there is no need to give someone else discretion over their account.

Short-term Traders

A short-term trader is an investor that is looking for brief, but powerful opportunities in the market place. They are willing to buy and sell over a very short period of time for a quick profit.

Short-term and options traders will find that the Hot Cycles in Part Three are incredible opportunities for making exceptional gains. Understanding the seasonal and monthly market trends will increase their chances of making profitable trades while decreasing the risks inherent with these activities.

In Summary, *Time In Time Out*:
- Can be used by any investor, from novice to professional
- Complements any short-term or long-term strategy that you may be using.

4

Calendar Investing: Who Will Tell You About It?

There have been numerous studies over the years that have analyzed the performance of the markets during different times of the year. The majority of these studies support our findings: investing in accordance with established seasonal trends is successful. While the results of these studies are not a secret, you would be hard-pressed to find out more information because they are not well promoted by high profile institutions.

The financial industry has very little to gain by encouraging people to be out of the market, and the truth is that it wants you "in the market" all of the time. The industry is entrenched with very traditional investment strategies and it may take a while for our system to impact the way business is done.

My broker has not told me

The full service brokerage industry has difficulty implementing this type of a system, so they may not want to tell you about it. In reality, a broker manages 300 to 500 clients and it would be impossible to contact them all in a timely fashion to get them in or out of the market. Even if they could call each client, the role of the broker is not to have clients sitting in cash during the bad months of the year. They are compensated for their time by selecting and trading stocks.

This is not meant to imply anything negative about brokers. After all, we were brokers and we understand the nature of the business. Most of our clients had no intention of taking a break from the market even if it was declining, preferring instead to focus on specific stocks that could hopefully defy the trend.

The dominant mindset of the financial industry is that stock-picking is the best investment method. Professionals believe that making good choices will prevail over a temporarily depressed market in the long-term, therefore, the use of timing is unnecessary.

This book will help you and your broker understand the nature of the market cycles and develop profitable trading strategies. Together, you can determine your action plan. This will complement the efforts of your broker, while maximizing your returns.

The mutual fund industry has not told me

The mutual fund industry has served the average person well in North America; making them better-off financially than most self-directed investors. Mutual fund managers have taught investors the value of investing in the stock market for the long-term and the ultimate rewards of doing so. Despite all of the investor educational efforts, the mutual fund industry has never directly addressed the seasonal volatility issue for their customers.

Fund companies employ bright managers who have worked in the financial industry for a number of years and have been first-hand witnesses to the seasonal trends. These managers understand that the market tends to rise and fall at certain times during the year, but they are unable to take any action, as they must follow the objectives of the fund.

If the manager has a mandate that allows flexibility in the amount of cash they are allowed to hold in the fund, then they have the freedom to decrease the stock holdings during the negative periods and increase the stock holdings in the positive times. Should the objective of the fund require being almost fully invested in stocks at all times, then the manager has no recourse but to deliver poor performance during a market decline. In addition, the problem of investors adding or redeeming money during volatile times, results in a situation where implementing any type of timing strategy is virtually impossible.

The mutual fund companies prefer that you buy and hold their funds *forever* because it is the only strategy that complements their business model. They do not want you to actively buy and sell throughout the year, because this adds to their costs and causes more work for their managers. As well, these companies collect management fees only when you are invested in their products, and not when you are sitting in cash.

We expect that fund companies will be slow to endorse calendar investing because it does not suit their method of doing business. The exception may be from the index fund industry because *Time In Time Out* fits so well with an index fund strategy (detailed in Part Two). When calendar investing products are offered, it will be done in an effort to appeal to the more astute consumer demanding a greater defensive approach to money management. After all, investors expect that "buy and hold" does not mean "buy and get killed" by being fully invested in a declining market.

Institutional Managers

Some institutional managers that manage pension funds or discretionary pools take advantage of calendar investing in a small way. They overweight their stock holdings during the best times of the year and underweight during the worst. Unfortunately, some of these managers are also restricted by the typical mandate of mutual funds, limiting the amount of cash the fund can hold. Institutional managers also find it difficult to make rapid changes in their large portfolios. This is especially true if they have to make a major change on a specific date.

The institutional managers that we have shown the *Time In Time Out* system to, have been excited by the identification of the trends. The prime reason is that they are usually compensated directly in relation to how their funds perform against major indices. If the manager beats the index which their fund is measured against, then they earn a performance bonus. It is not surprising that they are interested in the *Time In Time Out* system because of its ability to beat the index with less time exposure to the markets, and subsequently less risk.

In summary, few people will tell you about calendar investing because:

- It is difficult for brokers to implement calendar investing for all of their clients
- It is not compatible with the business plan of the mutual fund industry
- The financial industry does not approve of taking a break from the markets, since the industry wants you in the market all of the time.

5

Calendar Investing Criticisms—No Longer Valid

In the past, academics have written papers on the subject of market seasonality. Sometimes a newspaper would use the information for a column, but at the end of the column, they would usually state that there was a concern with the issues of taxation and transaction costs. There was also the concern that there was not enough investment product to effectively use a calendar strategy.

All of these concerns are no longer valid. First, investors now have huge 401(k) plans (RRSP's in Canada), and they can trade all they want in these accounts without any tax implications. For any taxable accounts, *Time In Time Out* is no less tax-efficient than any other systems in existence. Second, fee-based accounts and internet trading have driven transaction costs down to nominal levels. Third, there has been a proliferation of index products in recent years to make calendar investing simple.

Charging an Arm and a Leg?

Expensive commission fees used to be the strongest argument given by the "experts". At one time, commissions were regulated and transaction fees were in excess of 2% for both the buy and the sell. A huge investment gain was necessary to make a profit under these conditions. Commission charges have decreased substantially over the last few years, thanks in large part to the increased competition in the discount brokerage industry. There are some reputable companies even allowing investors to do all of their online trading for free, providing that they have $100,000 worth of investments with the firm. Other companies are now offering trades as low as $7 to $12 per trade. Cost is no longer the impediment it once was, and most people give it little thought these days.

Also, many full service brokerage firms now offer fee-based accounts, where clients are charged a flat rate per year instead of a per transaction charge. This concept has grown in popularity over the last few years as investors learn to appreciate the freedom of making decisions without additional costs. Implementing calendar investing can be done easily with a fee-based account. The end result is that the cost argument is now irrelevant.

The Inevitable Taxation

The second argument was that calendar timing triggered taxes when securities were sold every year. For most people, this is no longer an issue.

Years ago when this argument was first presented, 401(k) plans and RRSP's were not widely used by individuals like they are today. In recent times, investors have accumulated far more in their registered accounts than they have in taxable trading accounts, and they use their registered accounts more frequently. Our answer to this issue today, is to use your registered account for calendar investing and pay no taxes at all.

If you are going to use your taxable account, our system is as tax efficient as any other investment method that involves realizing gains on a yearly basis. Investors who are trading stocks on a short-term basis or holders of mutual funds that produce annual distributions will be familiar with this "pay as you go" taxation regime.

Buy and hold investors always believe that they are paying less tax on their gains than others because they are paying the tax less often. This can be misleading because the frequency of payment is a very small part of any comparison done between investment methods. Instead we suggest that buy and hold investors turn their attention to the issue of returns because this is where most of the taxation difference stems from. We have already shown that the buy and hold investors are not achieving the level of returns that our system produces, so it follows that they will not pay as much tax.

Paying tax on profits, whether derived from long-term investing or short-term investing, is preferable to paying no tax due to having no profits. Never let the "tax" tail wag the "investment" dog.

Buy and hold investors also believe that they are enjoying tax-free compounding on their investment by not triggering their capital gains. While there is logic to this argument, investors fail to understand that their unrealized tax liability is compounding at the same time. This can lead these investors to think that they are worth far more than they really are on an after tax basis. Sooner or later, there is a day of reckoning for everyone when a stock is sold or passes to the next generation and taxes must be paid. The tax bills can be far greater than ever imagined.

In our final analysis, we conclude that the taxation issue cannot be accurately compared between all of the different investment strategies due to the large number of variables to consider. The timeframe, taxpayer's bracket, and the taxation rate are all factors in the equation. Combining these would produce too many scenarios to detail here. Our intention is not to write about taxation, rather, we want to show you the money making potential of our system over other investment systems.

The best advice we can give you concerning taxation is to check with your tax advisor regarding your existing exposure to capital gains before implementing any changes in your strategy.

Not Enough to go Around...

The last criticism used to be that the lack of product on the market made calendar investing more difficult. Ten years ago, a consumer trying to replicate the index would have had the choice of buying a basket of blue chip stocks, or buying a large-cap mutual fund containing the same stocks. Neither was a great choice considering that the cost of individual stock trades was high, and most mutual funds were of the load variety (meaning high costs to buy or sell).

Since that time, a large number of products have been created to simplify the task of investing for everyone. Today, banks, trusts, life insurance companies and mutual fund companies that sell direct, offer families of no-load mutual funds; and quite a few of them also have a selection of index funds. Depending on the company that you deal with, calendar investing can be implemented at a very low cost.

Finally, index-based products such as SPY's, DIA's, QQQ's, and XIU's (TSE300) have been created to allow small investors to purchase the entire index selection of stocks in one convenient vehicle. These units are inexpensive to manage and trade, while offering the benefit of mirroring the return of the broad market. They are growing in popularity every year and currently enjoy an enthusiastic following.

Summing up, we see that *Time In Time Out*:
- Can be implemented at a low cost
- Can be used in non-taxable accounts
- Is easy to implement using the new index products.

Succeeding Where Traditional Methods Fail

This chapter explores the traditional methods used in investing, and how the principles of the *Time In Time Out* system helps alleviate the shortcomings of these methods. Regardless of how you make your investment decisions, calendar investing techniques add clarity and direction to your plan.

One of the most important principles for you to remember is that calendar investing is **not** market timing. There will be the inevitable comparisons drawn between our system and market timing systems because they both use buy and sell signals. Any comparison on this basis is too narrow and misses the fundamental difference.

The philosophy employed by *Time In Time Out* is quite simple: the dates used for entering and exiting the market are predetermined, based on historical precedents. Since these dates have worked in the past on a repetitive basis, it is highly probable that they will continue to work in the future. The degree of effectiveness, however, will be variable (just like the stock market). Due to the predetermined nature of our system, it can best be described as *proactive*. Before committing any money, *Time In Time Out* tells you exactly when you will be getting in and out of the market, as well as the reasons why you are doing so.

Contrast this method to any of the market timing systems you may have previously tried or are considering. Typically, their signals change from week to week or month to month, with absolutely nothing predetermined. It is possible for you to invest today because the market indicators appear positive, only to receive a sell-indicator next week. These other methods are in a constant state of flux, making them largely *reactive* in nature to varying market conditions.

The proactive approach of calendar investing versus the reactive approach of traditional methods is the largest differentiating factor between the two our system and the others. It is undoubtedly why calendar investing is so incredibly easy to use. While most timing methods require constant interpretation of ever-changing data, along with rapid deployment to be successful, *Time In Time Out* does not need frequent monitoring or adjusting. All that you need are just two actions per year in our Annual Cycle!

Market Timing: The "Gut Feel" Approach

Every investor has tried to anticipate the direction of the market at least once during their investment lives, and some continue to do it time and time again. All they are doing is listening to what their instincts are telling them at any moment, good or bad, and then acting on that urge. Basically, they are timing the market by their *gut feeling*.

For example, when investors are anxious about a market decline their bodies tense up, they feel stressed out, and their digestive systems do not function properly (the "gut" in gut feel). We have seen both investors and brokers alike suffer from nervous problems and ulcers as a result of market declines. Most investors respond to these feelings by going into a defensive mode in an effort to protect their capital. They sell their holdings and sit on cash to avoid any further pain or discomfort associated with their losses. They have taken action to seek relief from the symptoms of fear.

On the other end of the spectrum, investors enjoy a sense of calm and well-being when things are going well. Their happiness makes them feel confident and enthusiastic, so they tend to buy more holdings. They believe that by doing so, they will accumulate more money, and become more satisfied. Greed has clouded their financial perspective and they are no longer able to make objective investment decisions.

These emotions and instincts are the reason investors continually buy high and sell low. It does not matter if you are a very intelligent person or a very experienced investor; emotions can sabotage the best of us. They keep getting in the way of making sound, rational investment decisions that are easily made by other people who are detached from the situation. In fact, our instincts actually drive us to do the exact opposite of what we should be doing.

Many astute investors have commented on this in the past, but perhaps Sir John Templeton summed it up best when he was asked what he thought was the best time to buy stocks. His reply was to do so during a time of maximum pessimism. In the stock market, pessimism occurs when people feel absolutely defeated as they watch the value of their holdings plummet. The logical course of action is to buy more stocks when this happens because prices are low. Instead, investors are selling at a loss to relieve their anxiety, and suffer the consequences later.

It stands to reason that the reverse is also true. The most logical time to sell is during a time of extreme optimism. The problem with this concept is that investors are afraid of missing the last bit of profit during a period when markets are hitting consecutive new highs. Investors get lulled into a false sense of security, believing that their stocks will continue to advance at a fantastic rate forever. It goes against all instincts to sell in a rising market, yet this is precisely the time when investors must discipline themselves to take profits. Joseph Kennedy said a long time ago that he made a fortune selling too soon, because he sold during the rapidly rising market before the crash of 1929.

Investing is Counter-Intuitive

Only a minority of the investors attempting to time the market can cope with the emotional turmoil involved in the process. Given that the best time to buy is when you are afraid to and the best time to sell is when you do not want to, it is not a surprise that the majority of investors fail in their efforts to make the proper decisions. The investment industry continues to warn investors through reports that market timing does not work, and it should not be attempted.

From our observations, investors run into many obstacles that prevent them from achieving success using market timing. We want to outline a few of them here:

- **Are the markets undervalued or overvalued?**

This is a classic, and age-old debate. Most of the market timing literature produced passes judgement on the attractiveness of stocks and the market, based on the current relationship between earnings and prices (the P/E Ratio). Typically, the author justifies their position by relying on earnings growth projections compared with historical norms. Table 6.5 shows an example of two years in the last economic downturn, 1990 and 1991.

Table 6.5: Dow Jones Index Performance, with Price/Earnings Ratio

Year	Dow gain/loss	P/E Ratio
1990	-4.34%	15.3
1991	+20.32%	64.3

The year of 1990 produced some of the darkest days, as corporations were recording low earnings and the Dow index was dropping in anticipation of further poor results. The result was a relatively low Price to Earnings Ratio of 15 times earnings. This is a fairly low multiple, indicative of good value. Pessimism prevailed over the economy so there were few buyers to push prices up. In 1991, economic conditions started to improve and the market took off in anticipation of better profits, resulting in a high P/E Ratio for the market.

You can see that the P/E Ratio is simply a reflection of the situation at the time of measurement. If you attempt to speculate on the future value of the market from this measurement, you should know that it is an unreliable indicator since the P/E Ratio is going to fluctuate widely throughout the years depending on the current economic conditions and investor confidence.

The other problem often seen in determining the true value of the market at a given point in time is that it is a very subjective judgement. Using the same data at the end of 1998 for example, when the P/E ratio for the Dow was at 24, experts were divided in their opinions as to whether or not the market was fully-valued. Some argued that a value of 24 was at the high-end for the accepted range, and offered limited opportunity for further growth. Others believed that the economy was strong, and that the earnings growth would continue, therefore, there was more potential in the market.

The optimists won the argument as the market went on to advance 25% in 1999. The question that develops for the average investor is who to listen to: the optimists or the pessimists? Either one could be right.

When attempting to place a future value on the market, everyone has an opinion, but no one has a definitive guideline that works every time. If you are still trying to decide whether you should be buying or selling based on these opinions, expect to be wrong a good portion of the time.

In contrast to this anxiety-inducing timing method which is a constant attempt at guessing the direction of the market, consider how easily *Time In Time Out* would have handled both 1990 and 1991. Table 6.5 illustrated the following results:

1. The Dow returned -4.34% in 1990. Our system would have produced a gain of 19.74%.

2. In 1991, both methods had similar results: the Dow returned 20.32% and the Annual Cycle returned 20.65%.

You can see that our system beat the index without considering the value or direction of the market at any time.

- **Risk Management**

Risk Management involves devising a plan to protect capital. Typically, most investors fail to develop the necessary guidelines for buying and selling. Very often, they tend not to sell when the market is high, for fear of missing more profits. As well, they often miss the chance of buying low because they are already fully-invested and have no cash available. By not establishing their own guidelines, these investors are not allowing for any flexibility and they are realize very little benefit from their efforts of timing the market.

Time In Time Out incorporates risk-management principles by establishing firm buy and sell guidelines.

- **Trying to pick "The Bottom"**

An investor watches the market or a stock drop significantly, and then proclaims "This is the bottom. I'm buying!". The stock then drops another 15%, and the investor regrets their decision or even sells out in disgust. Guessing, instead of waiting for the market to bottom in its own time and then turn up, tends to be dangerous and quite expensive. There is not much more of a reward outside of pride by correctly picking the absolute bottom. *Time In Time Out* never claims to pick the absolute bottom of a market, rather the entry date is based on a historically low period in the year where most bottoms have occurred.

- **Not Realizing Profits**

Investors hesitate to sell for fear of missing the next market advance and more profits. As a result, they watch their capital shrink during the next inevitable market decline. *Time In Time Out* helps investors by keeping their expectations realistic. The fixed sell dates are established to ensure that profits are realized periodically.

Summing up market timing by "gut feel", we see that it:
- Usually does not work
- Is hard on the nerves and stressful
- Is counter-intuitive
- Makes buying low and selling high complex.

Market Timing: The "Guru" Approach

On the surface, you would think that following the advice of a seasoned market technician or analyst would be a less stressful way of timing the markets. This can be true because the expert employs a system that they developed over time and has demonstrated some merits. In application though, things can get complicated.

Some of the gurus are *analysts* who report their opinions based on the fundamentals. These are such measurements as P/E Ratios, earnings, interest rates, employment reports, book values, etc.

Though interesting, their information does little to add value to the average investor's strategies. The guru's advice usually has very little structure to provide investors with a systematic approach to follow. As a result, the investor is no better off after reading the guru's advice because little gets implemented. Investors must take the initiative to decide if they can devise a strategy based on all the information they have received.

The second group of experts are *market technicians*, a breed apart from the analysts as they do not care about fundamental indicators. Technicians confine their analysis to price history and volume data of the market or individual stocks, because they feel that this information is all that is required to understand the current investment climate. The underlying philosophy is that investors have already factored in all of the positive elements of a company or market, and the resulting price is an accurate reflection of the true value. Furthermore, the movement of price in certain patterns can be used as a predictive tool for future price movements (assuming that there are enough historical precedents available for comparison).

For more information on technical analysis, see your bookstore or library for any number of good books on the subject. One that we found particularly good was *The Streetsmart Guide to Timing The Stock Market* by Colin Alexander. Another source is the internet, where there are many sites devoted to technical analysis and market timing. A helpful site we found is Clearstation.com because it concentrates on teaching the basics of chart reading (www.clearstation.com/education).

Technical analysis can be a strong tool in the right hands because it provides a more disciplined framework for the investor. A buy or sell signal generated from technical analysis is usually much more definite and easier to implement than the vague recommendations of the fundamental analysts. There are some cautionary comments to pass on.

Guru's comments differ

Technical analysis is not a definitive science. You should expect a variety of opinions, even though each technician uses the exact same data to perform their analysis. For example, a website we consider very credible is Carl Swenlin's Decision Point (www.decisionpoint.com). There are a number of contributing analysts on this site with a variety of opinions. The analysts do not always focus on the same topics, nor do they share the same outlook. Do not expect any magical information about what will be the next event in the market, since each analyst is only offering an opinion. The good news is that you will have a large number of viewpoints to sample.

There are many viewpoints to choose from

If you were to use an internet search engine and type in "market timing" on the subject line, you would receive hundreds or thousands of hits. While it is impossible to review all of the sites listed, we did review a large number and concluded that it comes down to a case of buyer beware. The quality and quantity of information, opinions, fees and action plans vary widely.

Lots of talk, not many systems

Investors looking to follow the advice of a guru need direction with their financial plans. From what we have seen so far, investors cannot expect too much substance. There are many technicians willing to provide reports that outline great ideas, but only a small minority of them provide guidance on exactly how to take advantage of these ideas. The investment vehicles are not always spelled out, quantities relative to the total portfolio are lacking, and model portfolios are practically non-existent. Moreover, very few gurus have divulged their long-term performance track record, so investors have no idea if their chances of beating the index will be improved.

Summing up the "guru" approach, we see that:
- It has more structure than "gut feel", but not enough structure to make implementation easy
- There are many to choose from (perhaps too many)
- There are few models to follow
- Few gurus post track records
- Some subscriptions are expensive: Buyer Beware
- Following their advice can be confusing to the average investor.

The Stockpicking Bazaar

Picking your own stocks can be both fun and rewarding. Unfortunately, most investors who use this style for their investments end up with unsatisfactory results. This style involves a lot of risk, and often relies on having information that the general public does not possess. Potential percentage gains can be enormous, but so can potential losses.

Our time in the brokerage industry provided many insights into the advantages and disadvantages of stockpicking. This is a good time to review them so that you have the information to make an informed choice of whether or not you should be a stockpicker.

Stocks Versus the Index

Examining the outperforming and underperforming stocks in the Dow index over the past few years gives you an idea of how difficult it is to select the right companies, let alone do it consistently.

Figure 6.11 shows that over the past four years, only 56 stocks out of 120 beat the Dow on a total basis, for an average of 46%

success. In the past two years, the gap has widened as fewer stocks are beating the index. Table 6.6 details the numbers from Figure 6.11.

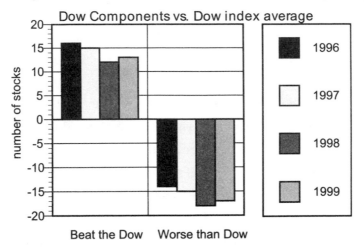

Figure 6.11: Comparing the Dow Components with the Dow Index

Table 6.6: Numbers of Dow Components and Dow index

	1996	1997	1998	1999
Beat the Dow	16	15	12	13
Worse than Dow	14	15	18	17

This is not a surprising result considering that the index is just a numerical average of the advances or declines of all 30 stocks in the index. If you were to choose five or ten stocks at random from the index, you might expect that your performance would come close to the index. This is a false assumption as success really depends on exactly which stocks you chose.

For example, in 1999 the best performing Dow stock was Alcoa with a 124% gain and the worst was Philip Morris with a 53% loss. This huge spread in returns illustrates the type of disparity that occurs every year. In 1998, Wal-Mart was at the top of the heap with a 107% return and Boeing at the bottom with a 32% loss.

If you picked the wrong Dow stocks, like Philip Morris, Goodyear (-42%), Sears (-26%), and Coke (-12%), there would be no chance of coming close to the index return, unless you had enough top performing stocks to off-set the losses of the underachievers. Chances are that you would not happen to choose all the losing stocks in any given year, but the possibility of doing so illustrates the need for diversification of your portfolio. This is precisely the reason why you hear time and time again that an investor should have twelve to fourteen stocks in their portfolio. With this level of diversification, the weighting in any one stock is not more than 7% to 8% of the total portfolio. This way, if something detrimental happens to one of your companies, you will not be subject to massive capital loss.

Most stockpicking investors today prefer to focus on a few select stocks in areas they understand, such as telecom or technology; rather than a more broadly based portfolio in many other fields such as oils, manufacturing or financial services. This puts them at much greater risk because they may find all of their stocks declining together if their chosen sectors turn negative.

These results are significant because they illustrate the unpredictably of the market. If the Dow Jones Industrial Average can experience this type of a spread in performance results, then you can be sure that the disparity between the winning and losing stocks is going to be even more dramatic in the smaller and lesser known indices.

Several good books are available on the subject of Dow stock selection using various techniques, and one of the best is *Beating The Dow* by Michael O'Higgins. Mr. O'Higgins outlines several strategies such as buying the lowest-priced, highest-yielding stocks every year in the expectation that these will recover the following year. The Motley Fool website is a good resource for selecting Dow stocks (www.fool.com) and also provides detailed history on the success of the various strategies.

How Have Professional Money Managers Performed?

You would think that mutual fund managers and institutional money managers could easily crush the Dow given the scope of the tools at their disposal. The sponsoring firms employ armies of analysts and portfolio assistants to help sort through the data on thousands of companies, in an attempt to select the absolute best prospects. Despite all of this time, money and effort, most professional mutual fund managers fail to beat the index.

According to Bethany McLean of *Fortune Investor*, only 11% of the managers beat the index over the past ten years and only 4% beat the index over the past fifteen years. Most of these managers maintain portfolios consisting of 100 of the best stocks they can find and which have an average annual turnover rate of 80% (this means 80% of the stocks are changed in a year). It seems only reasonable that they could find incredible opportunities that would outpace the index, but this is not the case over the long-term.

There are some good reasons for this divergence of performance by the managers. First, consider the overhead involved when paying the analysts and assistants, plus covering the cost of rent, computer systems and marketing. It is an expensive business to set up and operate before any money can be made. Next, money managers must limit the level of risk with clients' money. To do this, they must spread the money out over a large number of stocks. This dispersion actually increases as the amount of money managed increases. The more holdings the manager has, the more compromised their performance becomes. Although money managers try to beat the index, they are limited by their constraints.

Warren Buffett is undoubtedly one of the best investors in existence and is one of the few investors who has managed to beat the Dow. Mr. Buffett went on record in the 1993 Berkshire Hathaway Annual Report to state: "By periodically investing in an index fund, the know-nothing investor can actually outperform most investment professionals".

He went on to say: "If you want to make sure that nothing bad happens to you relative to the market, you should own everything. There is nothing wrong with that. It is a perfectly sound approach for somebody who does not know how to analyze businesses".

Using *Time In Time Out* with an index investing strategy can help you outperform most investment professionals.

What Resources Do You Have to Beat the Dow?

You might think that you have all of the information and the tools you need to beat the market, but do you? While there is a proliferation of information in the financial media, the sheer volume does little to aid sound decisions. Instead, it may only serve to confuse most people. Also, the real value of the information should be questioned. In a newspaper or television interview, have you ever seen a corporate insider give any first-hand information before it happens? Business transactions such as mergers, acquisitions and earnings surprises are never discussed before they happen, yet they are the elements that most frequently enhance stock value. The public will not be made aware of this information ahead of time, so do not expect to learn anything of true value easily or quickly from the media.

Are you able to make stockpicking decisions yourself or do you rely on the latest analyst recommendations, hoping for a real winner this time? If you follow the analysts, then you should know that they are notoriously bullish regarding the stocks they cover. From reports on over 6,000 companies in 1999, only 1.0% of the recommendations were "sells" according to Zack's Investment Research. The remainder of the reports were either buy or hold recommendations. This suggests that virtually all stocks are worthy of your attention and money, and a situation will certainly make your job of identifying superior companies a challenge. Besides, simply relying on analysts to make your picks is abdicating your responsibility for your money. If you want to blindly follow the advice of someone else, you may as well buy a mutual fund and just hope for the best.

While *Time In Time Out* cannot help you choose individual stocks, it can serve as a resource for trading them. The Annual Cycle shows you the high and low points of the year, so you can plan your buys and sells more productively. The Super Seven strategy that is part of the Hot Cycles also illustrates the strongest time to make a short-term trade.

Stockpicking as a lifestyle

In the past year or two, stockpicking has become a fascination for more investors than ever before, and in some cases, an obsession. It seems that everyone is trading their preferred companies online and talking about stocks around the water cooler at work. Raging bull markets have this effect.

The belief is that stockpicking gives us the chance to make the big hit— to buy a company that is going to make us rich. We have all heard the tales of someone buying Microsoft in the 1980's and now living in luxury. As a result, investors often try to make a big hit with speculative stocks. Even if they know that the chance of being correct is slim, they still want to play the game. It is similar to buying a lottery ticket where the odds are overwhelmingly against you; buying that ticket is still worth the few dollars you spend. If you are trying to hit the jackpot with speculative stockpicking, you should be comfortable losing the amount of money that you invest.

Stockpicking can become more than just an investment method. Some people choose it as a lifestyle because they are caught up in the excitement of getting rich. For many investors, the social implication of stockpicking is an important factor, but a key point to remember is that stockpicking is not all glamour. Stress and failed investments overwhelm many investors. As well, stockpicking becomes increasingly difficult when the bull market changes to a bear market.

If you have the time and the talent to do the necessary research required, maybe you can be a successful stockpicker. If you are lacking in these two elements, then you are kidding yourself about being able to beat the market index. After being in the business, we know how tough it is to consistently pick winners. Even if you are good at it, picking enough winners to build a diversified portfolio is very challenging.

Perhaps you are already immersed in the stockpicking mentality and want a break, but feel that you cannot completely give it up. In this case, try holding only a few companies you want to keep for a long time. Sell the rest of the stocks that you may not be sure of, and use the cash to implement the calendar investing system with an index strategy. *Time In Time Out* can help stockpickers who have doubts about many of their portfolio holdings and are actively seeking an alternative investment method.

Are You Emotionally Equipped?

"If you can't convince yourself 'when I'm down 25 per-cent, I'm a buyer' and banish forever the fatal thought 'when I'm down 25 percent, I'm a seller', then you'll never make a decent profit in stocks". Peter Lynch, *One Up On Wall Street*

Being a stock trader is hard on the nerves. You may already know this from experience, but to people new to the investing game, the emotions involved with stockpicking are just a mystery. With so many people caught up in the excitement of the market going up, there are bound to be some personal tragedies when the market turns down. Investors should be prepare for elevated anxiety due to increasing market volatility and large swings in investor sentiment.

Can Individual Stocks Escape Seasonal Downturns?

If you choose to be a stock trader, remember that the majority of stocks cannot escape the downward pull of the market during a negative time of the year. The opposite is also true; the majority of stocks increase during a positive time of year. Figure 6.12 illustrates the close seasonal correlation between the Dow index and 3M, a long-standing Dow component.

It is not important whether 3M has returned as much as the index in this comparison; rather, it is the harmony of the trends through the year we want you to notice. No stock will move in perfect balance with the index, but generally speaking, many stocks will tend to follow a similar trend to the index.

The following graph shows similarities in the peaks and troughs of 3M and the Dow. They occur at roughly the same time, but the magnitude may not be equal.

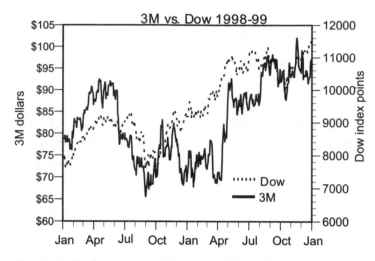

Figure 6.12: Comparison Between 3M and Dow Jones Index

Now consider the case of another Dow component. Figure 6.13 shows Hewlett Packard versus the Dow index at the buy date of the Annual Cycle.

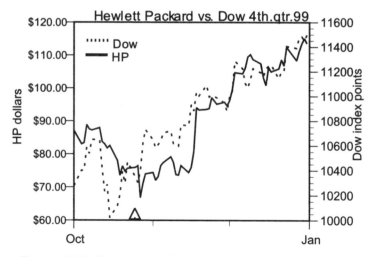

*Figure 6.13: Comparison Between Hewlett Packard and
Dow Jones Index*

Figure 6.13 illustrates two points:

1. First, Hewlett Packard bottomed at precisely the same time as the market, which is consistent with the historical average for the index.

2. Second, you can time your purchases and sales according to the buy and sell dates used for the *Time In Time Out* Annual Cycle.

In summary, stockpicking is a difficult strategy because:

- It leads to increased cost
- It can be stressful and time consuming
- Most stockpickers do not beat the index
- Stocks have seasonal trends similar to the market.

Buy and Hold

It would be inconceivable to suggest that buying and holding quality blue chip stocks has not proven to be a valuable method of investment. When hot sectors have given up, stock rotation tactics have gone cold and all other methods have failed, the entire financial services industry falls back on the argument that the buy and hold strategy is the tried and true method. While there is a degree of truth to this claim because it is based on comparisons with other methods, we believe that investors are never given the full story. Throughout this section we will give you the facts about buy and hold, so you can decide for yourself if this is the strategy for you.

In stating their case for buy and hold, the financial industry chooses to show examples of only the winning stocks, but ignores the remaining average or below average performers. The investing public is led to believe that they can buy and hold *anything* for a long time and make superior returns. Nothing could be further from the truth.

As we will show you, less than one-half of the stocks in the Dow index match or beat the index average in any given year.

The other problem we see all the time is that the financial industry rarely uses the Dow index in comparisons with their products and services. If they did, the buy and hold comparisons would be fair because the Dow is a universal performance benchmark that is very difficult to beat. We always compare our system to the Dow specifically for this reason. Investing $10,000 fifty years ago in the Dow index with buy and hold, would be worth $572,000 at the end of 1999 (without dividends), *or $1,046,000 using our system (without dividends and interest!). Time In Time Out* beat buy and hold by a substantial margin.

The Dow Index keeps changing

If an investor sat down on January 1, 1980 to choose Dow stocks to buy and hold, they would have had an impressive selection of blue chip companies to consider. The list would have included great companies that were household names: Sears, Goodyear Tire, Union Carbide, Woolworths, Bethlehem Steel, etc. Where are they now? Most companies on this list are still in business or have merged with another company, but they are neither in the Dow index nor are they the great leaders of industry they once were.

Indeed, *over one half of the stocks that were in the Dow in 1980 have been replaced* by the more modern names such as Home Depot, Microsoft, Hewlett Packard and Wal-Mart to name a few. *Over one third of the Dow stocks were replaced in the 1990's alone, at an even faster pace.* Change is a good thing in the long-term because it ensures that the Dow remains a reflection of the broad American economy. Table 6.7 shows the number of changes to the Dow index over the past eighty years.

Table 6.7: Changes per Decade of the Dow Jones Index

Year	# of Changes
1990's	11 changes
1980's	5 changes
1970's	3 changes
1960's	0 changes
1950's	5 changes
1940's	0 changes
1930's	23 changes
1920's	2 changes

In October of 1999, four stocks were changed in the index. The editors of the Wall Street Journal stated that the changes would make the Dow "more representative of the evolving U.S. economy" (www.dowjones.com), in which the fast-growing technology sector dominates. Some analysts said that this act was a rare change in policy, while others felt that the editors finally realized that the economy is truly entering a new age; the information age. This illustrates what was relevant to the Dow twenty years ago, is no longer relevant today. What is remarkable about the index changes in the 1990's is that *3 of the 4 companies added to the Dow were not even public companies in 1980.*

Investors using *Time In Time Out* and index products, should be ecstatic with these changes. They keep the Dow timely and relevant, which in turn leads to superior performance. For all other investors, it presents a formidable challenge. How do you beat an index that keeps changing? It is like trying to hit a moving target. The buy and hold method will have a difficult time keeping pace.

The world has changed and along with it, the way business is done. More index changes should be expected in the future, and perhaps at an accelerated pace. Who knows which companies out of today's blue chip components will be deleted from the Dow in the next decade? To illustrate how business and the economy have changed through the decades, Table 6.8 shows of all the stocks deleted from the Dow since 1920.

Table 6.8: Deletions and Additions to the Dow Jones Index

Date Deleted	Company Deleted	Company Added
01-11-99	Sears	Home Depot
01-11-99	Goodyear	Intel
01-11-99	Chevron	Microsoft
01-11-99	Union Carbide	SBC Communications
17-3-97	CBS (Westinghouse)	Citigroup(Travelers)
17-3-97	Texaco (Texas Corp.)	Hewlett-Packard
17-3-97	Bethlehem Steel	Johnson & Johnson
17-3-97	Woolworth	Wal-Mart
06-5-91	Navistar International (International Harvester)	Caterpillar
06-5-91	USX (U.S. Steel)	Disney
06-5-91	Primerica (American Can)	JP. Morgan
12-3-87	Inco Limited (Intternational Nickle)	Boeing
12-3-87	Owens-Illinois	Coca-Cola
30-10-85	American Brands (American Tobacco B)	McDonald's
30-10-85	General Foods (Postum Inc)	Philip Morris
30-8-82	Manville Corporation (John's Manville)	American Express
29-6-79	Chrysler	IBM
29-6-79	Esmark(Swift&Company)	Merck
09-8-76	Anaconda	Minnesota Mining & M
01-6-59	National Steel	Aluminum Company
01-6-59	American Smelting	Anaconda
01-6-59	Corn Products Refining	Esmark (Swift&Co)
01-6-59	National Distillers	Owens-Illinois
03-7-56	Loew's Inc.	International Paper
14-3-39	IBM	AT&T
14-3-39	Nash Kelvinator (Nash Motors)	United Technologies (United Aircraft)
20-11-35	Bordon	DuPont
20-11-35	Coca-Cola	National Steel
13-8-34	United Technologies (United Aircraft)	National Distillars

Table 6.8: Deletions and Additions to the Dow Jones Index

15-8-33	Drug Inc.	Corn Products Refining
15-8-33	International Shoe	United Technologies
26-5-32	Liggett & Myers	American Brands
26-5-32	Hudson Motor	Coca-Cola
26-5-32	Mack Trucks	Drug Inc.
26-5-32	National Cash	RegisterIBM
26-5-32	Texas Gulf Sulpher	International Shoe
26-5-32	Paramount Publix	Loew's Inc.
26-5-32	Radio Corp.	Nash Kelvinator
26-5-32	United Air Transport	Procter & Gamble
18-7-30	American Sugar	Borden
18-7-30	Goodrich	Chevron(StandardOil)
18-7-30	American Brands (American Tobacco B)	Eastman Kodak
18-7-30	Atlantic Refining	Goodyear
18-7-30	Curtiss-Wright	Hudson Motor
18-7-30	General Railway Signal	Liggett & Myers
18-7-30	Nash Kelvinator(Nash Motors)	United Air Transport
29-1-30	North American	Manville Corporation
14-9-29	Wright Aeronautical	Curtiss-Wright
08-1-29	Victor Talking Machine	National Cash Register

This information may shock some people who think the Dow is "old fashioned" or not representative of the modern American economy. In reality, the index has been carefully adjusted to encompass more new economy and global companies, especially throughout the 1990's. This makes the index an excellent reflection of the domestic economy.

To see if the buy and hold approach is worthwhile, let us look at how some of the stocks that were deleted from the Dow have performed relative to the index over the past twenty years.

Table 6.9 lists the total growth of the companies in Figure 6.14. All results are over the 20-year period, and exclude dividends.

Table 6.9: Comparison of Dow Jones and Deleted Components

Dow	Bethlehem	Inco	Goodyear
1,294%	-43%	110%	829%

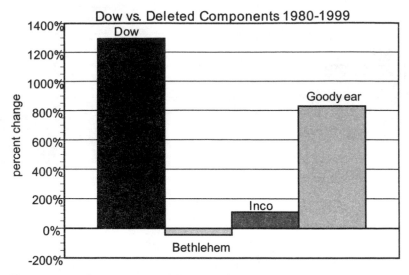

Figure 6.14: Comparison of Deleted Companies and the Dow

The three stocks used for this comparison were chosen from a larger list of the sixteen deleted companies based on the data available for the full twenty years. Some of these stocks have performed very poorly when compared to the Dow.

Whatever the reason for their deletion, it is clear that investors who selected these stocks twenty years ago to "buy and hold forever", have not received great returns on their money. They probably regret their choices today when they see other stocks performing at the level of the Dow or better.

Assessing the index changes

If you are thinking of buying Dow companies today with the intention of holding them for the next twenty years, which ones would you buy and how do you know they will be in good financial shape ten years from now? By all means, if you love a particular company in the Dow, go ahead and add it to your portfolio, but do not bet your retirement on it. How can anyone foresee which stocks will be in the next group of non-performers ten or twenty years from now? Also, how can anyone know the group of stellar performers that will be added to the Dow over the same timeframe?

Instead of selecting individual stocks, our system uses the Dow index products to ensure that you always own a diversified portfolio of modern companies. These products further provide the other major benefits such as low cost and simplicity of use, discussed throughout this book.

What about the Dow Survivors?

To give you a relative comparison of the stocks that have remained in the Dow index since 1980, the following bar graph shows their growth over the same twenty year period.

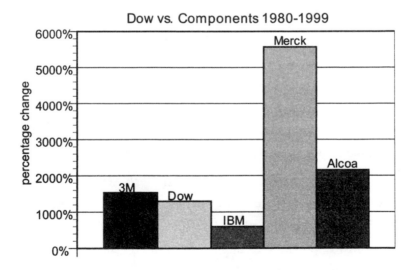

Figure 6.15: Comparison of Dow Jones and Present Components

The percentage growth numbers from Figure 6.15 are:

Table 6.10: Comparison of Dow Jones and the Present Components

Dow	3M	Merck	IBM	Alcoa
1,294%	1,531%	5,567%	594%	2,153%

This table looks different from Table 6.9, which showed the first group of stocks that were deleted from the index. The stocks listed in Table 6.10 were all the latest *additions* to the Dow just before 1980. In this case, 3 out of 4 additions have outperformed the index over the twenty years.

If you had picked these stocks in January of 1980, you would be wealthy today, but how would you have known to pick these stocks instead of the previous group of deleted stocks? Would you have picked these companies or would you have remained faithful to the tried and true stocks of the day, the ones that were stuck in the old economy?

Do you still believe you can buy and hold *anything* and retire a millionaire? The inevitable conclusion we have reached is that ***buying and holding stocks can help you beat the index in the long run, but only if you have the right stocks!***

The best solution is to use our system with an index product. In doing so, you will have no concern about owning individual stocks which may perform at an inferior level to the index, which is always current.

Using Time In Time Out With Stocks

The *Time In Time Out* system works to increase performance over the buy and hold method. We took the twenty years of data for 3M from the previous example and applied the Annual Cycle to check for an improvement. Using the calendar investing timeframes to buy and sell every year, *as opposed to buying and holding,* resulted in the next table.

Table 6.11: Comparison of Buy and Hold and Time In Time Out
Returns for 3M, over the years of 1979 to 1999

	Buy and Hold	*Time In Time Out*
Cumulative return	1393%	1510%

This scenario was run from October 1979 to July 1999 and corresponds to our Annual Cycle detailed in Part Two. All results exclude dividends and interest, so it is a straight comparison of the growth between the two systems. You can see that the returns were definitely enhanced by using our system, and it would certainly make a difference to your long-term financial well-being.

3M is not an isolated example by any means and is representative of the majority of Dow stocks in its seasonality. You can use our strategy with any large blue chip company you own for enhanced returns. If you wanted to sell some of your existing stock holdings to raise some cash, the best time to do this is while prices are high. Our seasonal indicators can serve as a practical guideline for receiving maximum value. Likewise, if you had cash and wanted to add to your stock holdings, our guidelines show you when prices are low.

But are you really a Buy and Hold Investor?

Many people believe they are buy and hold investors. We offer some questions you can ask yourself to determine whether or not you are a true buy and hold investor:

- Do you focus on the future potential of your investment or on its present value?
- Do you detach yourself from large swings in the market, or do you tend to become worried, confused or tempted by the value of your holdings?

- Do you have total faith in your current holdings, or do you have doubts about the long-term viability of what you own?
- Do you tend not to look at the value of your portfolio from year to year, or often check the value and measure performance?

If you have chosen the first part in each question then you likely are a true buy and hold investor. Although you may be comfortable with a buy and hold strategy, using our system will increase your profits.

If you have chosen the second part in each question perhaps you are not really a buy and hold investor. *Time In Time Out* will eliminate any of the doubts and fears you may have with a buy and hold strategy, while assuring that your performance stays competitive.

In summary, we see that:

- Buy and hold works well, but only if you own the right stocks
- Roughly one half of the Dow stocks do not achieve the index average
- The composition of the Dow index changes all of the time (the Dow itself is not a buy and hold strategy)
- Using calendar investing can improve individual stocks performance
- Using an index strategy can relieve the uncertainties inherent with individual stocks.

Part 2

The Best Six Months of Your Life

This part of the book details the Annual Cycle of the *Time In, Time Out* system, indexing tools you need to implement it and recommended portfolio constructions. Highlights include:

- **The Annual Cycle:** the cyclical patterns of the market over the past 46 yearly cycles, the returns produced by the Annual Cycle compared with the Dow index, and the best time to be invested in of the market.
- **The Tools You Need:** the numerous products that can be used when implementing the *Time In, Time Out* strategy in any type of account.
- **Build Your Portfolio:** an example of how to construct the equity portion of your holdings.

The Annual Cycle

The Annual Cycle is the foundation upon which the *Time In Time Out* system is built. During the course of developing the Annual Cycle, we discovered two distinct approaches: one for conservative investors and one for aggressive investors. Both of these will be explained in detail in this chapter and you will be given guidelines as the most appropriate approach for your needs.

Our objective was to find a yearly pattern that would allow an investor to significantly increase their rate of return over the Dow Jones index, by using predetermined buy and sell dates each and every year. In doing so, any investor could easily implement the system, while enjoying superior investment performance.

The Annual Cycle resembles the buy and hold approach to investing by keeping activity to a minimum throughout the year, and by participating in the market during the most positive times every year. However, the key difference between the two investment methods lies in the Annual Cycle's avoidance of the negative period of the year. If an investor wants to beat the Dow, the easiest way to do this is to be selective about the times they invest and the times they do not invest.

If the patterns of the market were obvious, every investor would already be following them. This is not the case. Before we developed the *Time In Time Out* system, it was very difficult to identify or quantify these patterns with any certainty. After spending a year analyzing data, writing programs and measuring results, we were able to create a guide to understanding the trends clearly.

Seasonality has always existed in the stock market but until now has remained elusive. By analyzing the Dow Jones index data from 1953 to 1999, it is now possible to give investors one optimal buy date and two optimal sell dates for the year. What you are about to learn is not yet common knowledge, so you will have a real advantage over others who are trying to beat the Dow.

The picture below is a screen shot of the program we developed as part of the research for this book. We incorporated a number of long-term and short-term analysis tools into the program, which you can learn more about on our website (www.upwave.com).

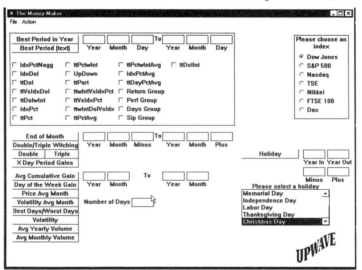

Figure 7.16: Interface for the Data Analysis Program

Comparing Percentages

When reviewing the data and presenting the results for this book, great care was taken to measure index performance in terms of *percentage change*, and not *gross point change*. This method was chosen to provide consistency across the decades and a meaningful comparison of seasonal movements. For example, ten years ago a 120 point movement in the Dow was a large gain or loss; approximately 5% of its value. Today, that same 120 point movement is only a 1% gain or loss, and is practically a daily occurrence.

How Successful Is This System?

The Annual Cycle generates higher historical returns with less risk and volatility, in comparison with buying and holding the Dow Jones index. By testing the system from 1953 to 1999, we show that a conservative investor would have outperformed the Dow by **45%**, and an aggressive investor by **98%**. These results are based on market returns only, *without any dividends or interest factored in!* The results are detailed later in this chapter.

Is It Simple?

Time wise, the Annual Cycle requires only fifteen minutes a year. You only have to decide on how much of your capital you want in the Dow index, buy the index in the fall and sell in the spring or summer on the exact dates given. It really is that easy. There are no graphs to look at, no valuation models to consider and no financial fundamentals of particular companies to worry about. You are either in the Dow index or in cash, making T-Bill / money market interest returns.

What About Asset Mix?

From a financial planning perspective, it is important to view the calendar investing system as the equivalent of owning any equity investment. This means that you must decide on your asset allocation first, taking into consideration your own unique situation. After this is done, you determine how to make your equity investment which would include *Time In Time Out*. We are confident that you will find many benefits with our system, but please remember that **it cannot work miracles**! If the market goes down while you are invested in the index with our system, you should be prepared to lose money.

If you are unsure of the proper asset mix to use, there are a number of good books to read for advice. Better yet, you should consult with a professional CFP practitioner (**see Appendix G: About Financial Planning** for more information).

How To Use This Chapter
The balance of this chapter will take you through the Annual Cycle in the same progression as it was developed, which will help you understand the reasons behind the Annual Cycle. The major topic headings are:

- Finding the Start Date for the Annual Cycle
- Determining the Time Out Date
- Results for the Conservative Exit Date
- Determining the Aggressive Time Out Date
- Results for the Aggressive Exit Date
- Analyzing the Time Out Cycles
- Examining the Individual Months of the Year.

Finding The Start Date for the Annual Cycle

When a long-term graph of the Dow Jones index or any other index is first viewed, it is difficult to discern any meaningful patterns. The movements usually appear random in nature with peaks and valleys scattered over the years. Figure 7.17 illustrates this point using a graph of the Dow index for the years of 1997 to 1999.

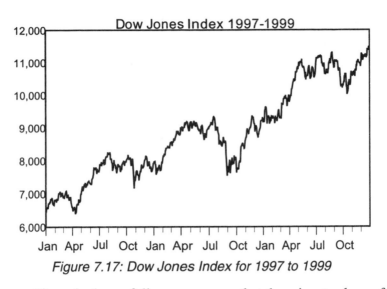

Figure 7.17: Dow Jones Index for 1997 to 1999

If you look carefully, you can see that there is a tendency for the peaks to occur around the same time of year. Similarly the lows tend to occur at roughly the same time every year, but the lowest point is often unclear. We noticed this problem when we started our research and concluded that long-term graphs were inadequate because the market movements became vague. The visual impact of percentage changes diminished as the magnitude of the Dow index grew. As the index increased through the years, the scale of values became very large, making the market changes throughout history less pronounced.

To solve this problem, we used graphs of average percentage movement over several different terms. For example, we derived the 25-year average as follows. For each year, we calculated the cumulative daily percentage gain from January 1st until the end of the year. We then averaged each of the 25 individual values for each day of the year, to produce an average yearly graph. The same general method was applied for any average data in this chapter.

Figure 7.18 illustrates how the average calendar year for the Dow performed over 25 and 46 years. This information was critical to our analysis of the high and low points that occur in an average year, and made the trends easier to identify.

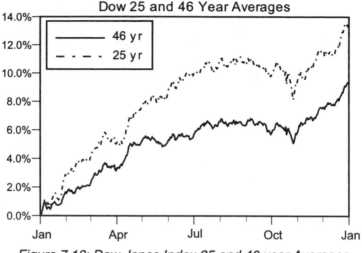

Figure 7.18: Dow Jones Index 25 and 46 year Averages

Identifying The Fall Buy Signal

Looking at Figure 7.18, it would be easy to assume that the best time to buy into the market index is at the beginning of the year on January 1st. The index value appears to be lowest at that time because that is where the trendline starts. *When using these graphs, the pattern of change is more important to note than the absolute value. What you really want to look for is a period of time where there is a sharp downtrend, followed by a steep uptrend. This makes an excellent buying opportunity.* This graph shows that there is a pronounced "dip" in the trendline during the month of October, which was not surprising.

From our experience in the investment industry, we knew that some months of the year did not perform as well as the others. October has often been characterized by uncertainty, corrections and crashes, so it was a logical place to start our search for a good time to buy. Since we were using average data going back many years, there was concern that the dip seen in October may not be representative of more modern trends. Figure 7.19 shows the five, ten, and fifteen year averages.

As you can see from this graph, the trends for shorter term averages remained similar to longer term averages, but with higher returns and more volatility. This supports the long-term trend of a decline in October.

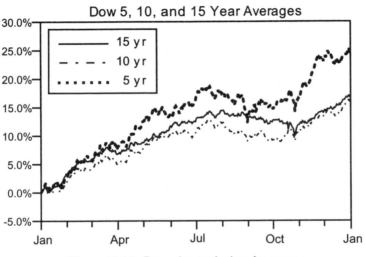

Figure 7.19: Dow Jones Index Averages

Volatility Supports the Trends

The average Dow index movement during the year is compelling evidence of seasonality, but the seasonal trends become pronounced when market volatility is also viewed. Figure 7.20 shows the average yearly volatility since 1953, expressed in average annualized standard deviation. This is a measurement of the relative rate at which prices are moving up and down, in comparison with their average.

Periods of high volatility indicate uncertainty in the market as prices are rising or falling in extremes. Periods of low volatility indicate a steadier rate of price appreciation or a more stable trend.

During the average year since 1953, market volatility has been relatively calm from the beginning of the year through to the spring or summer months. Volatility then surges in August through October. Finally, it returns to normal levels and drops to a low reading in the late fall.

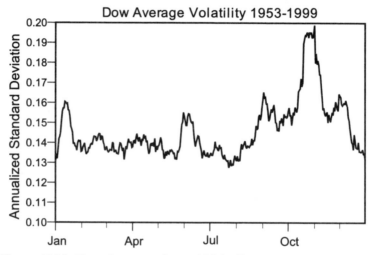

Figure 7.20: Dow Average Annual Volatility with 10-day Lookback

This information served to reinforce the decision to look for a start date in October. There was an obvious peak in the volatility trend late in the month that corresponded to the dip in the price trendline seen in previous graphs. The next step was to study the relationship between the price and volatility trends to see if there was a clear indication of an annual market bottom.

Figure 7.21 illustrates how the market tends to advance in value while volatility is low. At the point where the two plot lines first intersect, volatility is at its lowest level while the market is peaking in value. This is a classic pattern of a strong, overall market advance.

After a peak in July, prices start to decline while volatility starts to increase. This trend continues to build until a peak in volatility and a low point in price occur at the end of October. This trend is a general correction where falling prices inflate the volatility reading.

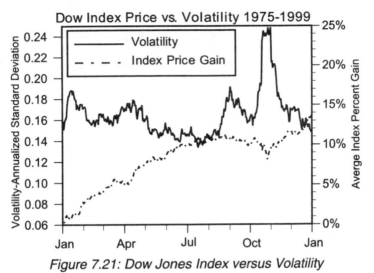

Figure 7.21: Dow Jones Index versus Volatility

From the end of October to the end of the year, prices stage a strong advance while volatility drops dramatically. This indicates a reversal of the negative price trend to a positive price trend, and the start of a new market rally. In fact, where the two plot lines intersect a second time at approximately December 1st in Figure 7.21, the market is usually enjoying one of the most euphoric times of the year.

This historical information effectively illustrates the two elements of risk and reward on a single graph, and explains the two parts of our system very well:

- The best time to be in the market is during a period of low volatility with steady price appreciation. This is the "Time In" portion of the year.
- The best time to be out of the market is during a period of rising to high volatility with choppy to declining prices. This is the "Time Out" portion of the year.

Zeroing In on the exact Time In Date

Graphs of average market percentage gains over the long-term proved to be an excellent indicator, as well as the price/volatility comparison. They illustrated that the end of October was the best time to examine more closely for a specific buy date. We "zoomed in" on the 120-day period centered around the end of October to determine exactly the best day to use as a buy date for the Annual Cycle. Figure 7.22 shows the 25 and 46 year averages.

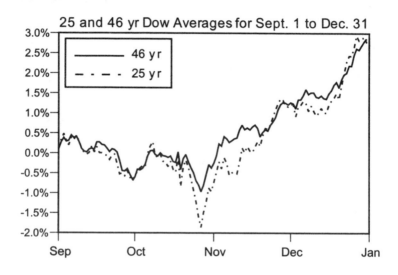

Figure 7.22: Dow Index Long-term Average over 120 Days

From this long-term average data, it was apparent that the last several days of October formed the actual bottom of the market. We then looked at more recent data to be sure that the trend had not changed over the past fifteen years. The next graph, Figure 7.23, was prepared using the five, ten and fifteen year averages.

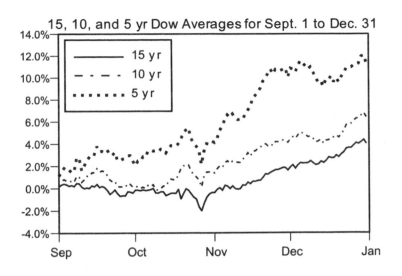

Figure 7.23: Dow Jones Index Average over 120 Days

Since these numbers are averages it was expected that the graphs would look alike, but the similarities were striking. Notice, however, the degree of change in the five year average. It shows much larger changes in value during the short-term, but the dip in the trendline is not as negative. Nonetheless, all of these indicators pointed to selecting a date that was three or four days before the October month end. It was possible to further narrow the exact buy date down to October 27th, 28th, or 29th, without any other supporting data.

We then turned our attention to an examination of individual years to see how widely they varied from the average. It was important to verify that there was very little deviation from the average because the start date was intended to be a low risk selection. That meant we were looking for a date that came after most of the market bottoms had occurred. It was important to find a date that worked well over the course of many years, realizing that it could not be expected to work *every* year. Figures 7.24, 7.25 and 7.26 use groups of three individual years, each from the past two decades to illustrate how each year performed around the estimated buy dates.

Examining the individual years, the pattern of market bottoms was found to be very consistent. For example, Figure 7.24 shows that in the past three years, a prominent trough was noted in late October for 1997 and 1999. In 1998, the bottom was seen earlier in October. This finding supports the data of the average years previously seen.

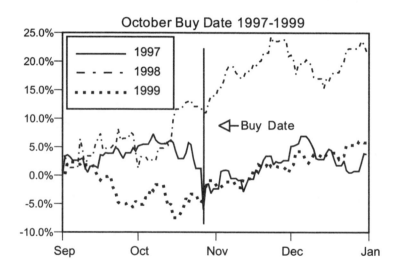

Figure 7.24: Examined Buy Dates for 1997 to 1999

Figure 7.25 shows how 1995 and 1996 experienced pullbacks in October, and rebounded from the end of the month to start new rallies. In 1992, the market bottomed earlier in the month.

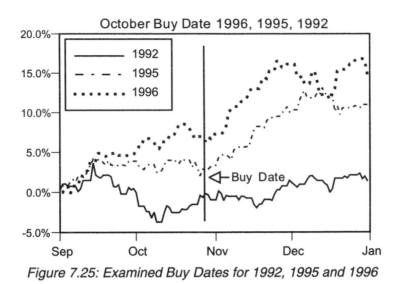

Figure 7.25: Examined Buy Dates for 1992, 1995 and 1996

Figure 7.26 includes 1981 and 1989 which conformed to the late October trend, as well as 1987 which experienced a massive decline prior to the end of October.

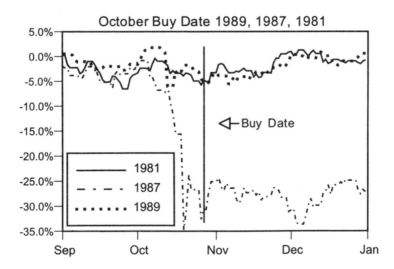

Figure 7.26: Examined Buy Dates for 1981, 1987 and 1989

In certain individual years, it would have been possible to buy at a slightly lower level than the proposed buy dates. The problem with doing so is that there is not enough consistency in the patterns over the 46 years of history to justify buying earlier.

Furthermore, the buy dates targeted thus far avoid the risk of having the market decline further after you buy. From our research, the index rarely goes lower after the end of October. We concluded that a buy date at the end of October offers the least risk.

Pinpointing the Buy Date

To verify that the indications from the previous graphs were correct and to select a single buy date, the eight days prior to November 1st were input into our program as possible buy dates. For the purpose of this analysis, we used a constant exit date (discussed later in this chapter). Since the bottom of the market occurred on a slightly different date every year, we needed to run our program to find out which date consistently produced the best returns. The model calculated returns for each scenario, using one of the eight possible buy dates and the fixed sell date. To be consistent with the long-term view already used, we studied the period from 1953 to 1999.

Table 7.12: Finding the Exact Entry Date

Buy Date	$ Cumulative Return	% Average Annual Return	Return Ratio	Performance Ratio
October 24	4,328,783	9.12	109	203
October 25	4,589,516	9.27	115	217
October 26	4,988,908	9.49	125	237
October 27	5,354,205	9.67	134	255
October 28	**5,805,937**	**9.88**	**145**	**276**
October 29	5,476,568	9.72	137	263
October 30	4,807,736	9.37	121	234
October 31	4,208,957	9.04	106	205
November 1	4,387,063	9.14	110	215

The $ Cumulative return and % Average Annual Return refer to the cumulative gain of the Annual Cycle, assuming the same entry and exit dates each year.

We compared average rates of return generated by each potential buy date, as well as total dollars returned. Using $100,000 as the initial investment, Table 7.12 shows the final values for each of the potential buy dates.

It was amazing to see the difference in performance between days grouped so closely together. The 5-day period from October 26th to the 30th produced results that were vastly superior to the days before and after this period. This illustrates that the dip in the market seen on the graphs is truly an outstanding buying opportunity.

The 28th day of October yielded the best results overall. Consider the impact of delaying the buying decision until November 1st. If an investor were to do so, the average annual rate of return would have been almost 0.7% less, which over the years would have yielded over **$1 million less**. *That's a $250,000 penalty for every day the purchase was delayed!*

We would like to explain some of the terms that have been used to express the results used in Table 7.12. These terms will continue to appear in the tables and graphs throughout the rest of this chapter.

What Does Return Ratio Mean?

Return Ratio is our measurement devised to indicate how well the *TITO* system has done, relative to the Dow index on a buy and hold basis. It reveals what percentage of the total Dow gain has been realized by achieving gains in the Time In period and avoiding losses during the Time Out portion of the cycle. Any Return Ratio over 100 indicates that the Annual Cycle has gained more than the Dow index on a buy and hold basis.

As an example, the Dow index returned 16.8% between October 28th, 1997 and October 28th, 1998. At the same time our system would have produced 30.4%, resulting in a Return Ratio of 198 (98% better than the Dow). This was possible because the Time In period sold out of the market at a higher level than the closing level of the Dow for that period. The calculations do not include dividends or interest.

Relating this information to Table 7.12, you can see how the number goes well over 100% for each day in the 9-day period. This reaffirms that this segment of the year presents a great chance to beat the index by a large margin. For the date of October 28th, the Return Ratio is 145 on a cumulative basis, beating the Dow by 45%!

A further enhancement: Performance Ratio

The 145 Return Ratio discussed previously is a substantial result, but the fact that it was achieved by being in the market for approximately one half of the year, makes it exceptional (discussed in the next section, **Determining the Time Out Date**). The Performance Ratio takes the timeframe into account by dividing the Return Ratio by the time participation of the measured period. For example, a Return Ratio of 145 is divided by the participation rate of 52.4% (the amount of time that you are in the market), which yields a Performance Ratio of 276. This ratio of 276 means that the measured Time In period is nearly three times as efficient in generating returns than the index on a buy and hold basis.

The Final Selection of the Buy Date

The ultimate day to be entering the market and starting the Time In portion of the Annual Cycle is **October 28th**. Since the calculations used in Table 7.12 include the performance for the 28th, this means you **must be in the market on this day** to take advantage of the strong advance that typically starts at this time.

Depending on the investment vehicle you choose, your options may be limited. For example, if your investment vehicle is a mutual fund, you must place your buy order the day before to ensure that the transaction will be done at the closing price of October 27th. If you are using index shares, the best way to ensure that all gains occurring on the 28th are captured, is to purchase them fifteen minutes before the close of the market on October 27th. If this is not possible, you have the ability to buy them when the market opens on the 28th.

There will be times when the 28th falls on a weekend and the market is closed. When this occurs, the buy date is the Friday before the 28th.

Do not be deterred if it seems like a really bad time to go into the market! Periods marked with high volatility and a sharp dip in price usually produce anxiety and pessimism, and the newspapers tend to be full of negative headlines about the market. Typically, a sharp correction in the index has occurred in September and October that has shaken investor confidence.

Although it may seem to be a poor time to invest, it is actually the best time. You will truly be "buying low" when other investors are still selling. Knowing that you are acting rationally based on historic data allows you to remain objective and confident during this time. The Time In period tends to gather momentum shortly after the buy date.

The Start of the Time In Cycle (November to January rally)

To further illustrate the importance of the October 28th buy date, revisit Figures 7.18 and 7.19 and look at what happens immediately following that date. We call this the start of the new investing year because November, December and January typically lead to strong rallies in the market and account for a large portion of the yearly gains.

Whether caused by relief from the previous negative period or a large inflow of pent-up money entering the market, the rally from the end of October to end of January is spectacular. From our research, it emerged as one of the best periods of the year.

We call this period the 100-Day Cycle because it runs for approximately 100 calendar days, from October 28th to February 4th of the next year. You will learn about this cycle in Part Three of the book, as it is one of the Hot Cycle strategies. From 1953 to 1999, this timeframe has produced daily performance gains that are approximately three times greater than the average daily gains of a buy and hold strategy.

To put the 100-day Cycle into perspective, consider that the average gain for this period is 5.9% over the past 46 years, compared with the average yearly gain for the Dow index of 9.62%. This means that the 100-day Cycle accounts for **61% of the average yearly gain**. What is most impressive about this result is that it is achieved by *participating in only 27% of the calendar year*! The gain is divided by the participation rate, to yield a Performance Ratio of 218. The bottom line is that the 100-Day Cycle is *twice as efficient at generating returns than buying and holding the Dow index.*

Does October 28 work with other indices?

The S&P500, Nasdaq, and the Canadian TSE300 all show very similar patterns to the Dow over the past fifteen years. Figure 7.27 is a comparison of all four major North American indices, showing their trends. This graph is not intended to compare the performance of each index to one another. Rather, the graph is meant to illustrate that similar seasonal trends are apparent in all of the major indices. However, the performance of each index will vary.

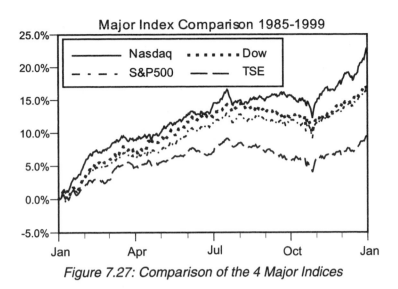

Figure 7.27: Comparison of the 4 Major Indices

Going back further in history, the Dow and the S&P500 can be compared from 1953 to 1999. Figure 7.28 shows how the pattern is virtually identical for both indices. In fact, it is difficult to tell the difference between them in places.

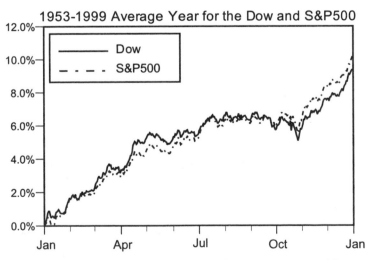

Figure 7.28: Dow Jones Index and S&P500 Average Years

The previous two graphs show that you can to use any index you want when implementing the *Time In Time Out* system because they all follow a similar seasonal direction, but the returns for each index will vary.

Determining The Time Out Date

Identifying the exit date for the Annual Cycle proved to be a much more complex task than selecting the buy date. Throughout history, there have been many different events that have influenced the movements of the market and created varied patterns. The research illustrated that the spring and summer months were full of such variances, making the task of selecting an optimal exit date challenging.

In some years the market peaked early in April or May, followed by a decline in early summer. In other years, the market peaked later in July or August with a pullback from August to October. In a few of the years, the market barely paused during the summer.

Recalling the volatility/price analysis of Figure 7.21, volatility was at a very low reading and price was at a very high reading during the months of May to July. This was a logical place to start the investigation for peak values, and therefore exit dates for the Annual Cycle. To analyze this period further, we turned to long-term average data to narrow the search.

Figure 7.29 shows the 5, 15 and 45 year averages for the Dow Jones index, from November 1st to October 31st. Notice that the start date for the yearly graph has been adjusted to November 1st in order to see the trend of our newly defined investing year more clearly. November is the closest full month to the established entry date, so we can use November 1st to start the graph in order to accurately depict the peaks and troughs of the year.

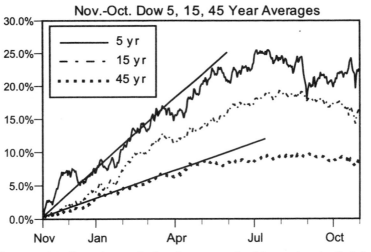

Figure 7.29: Dow Jones Index Averages for November to October

Two observations can be made examining this graph:

- The first observation is that there are prominent peaks in the 5 and 15 year averages in July, but the exact days are unclear. In the 45-year graph, the peaks are not as prominent but appear to be closer to May 1st.

- The second observation is how the market actually behaves on average in a year. The majority of the yearly gains occur from either the November to May period or the November to July period, depending on the trendline viewed. This is shown by the strong and extended upward movements in the first half of the graph. Then, depending on which average you select, the market flattens through the summer months and declines in the last quarter of the graph.

Figure 7.29 illustrates that the strong advance runs out of momentum in early May, and is completely exhausted by July. This means that the May 1st to the July 31st timeframe is an ideal choice for selling.

Scaling the Peaks

We needed more conclusive data before selecting the exit dates, so each individual year from 1950 to 1999 was examined to see exactly where a peak in value occurred. Since we have established that the period from May 1st to July 31st is the best time to sell, any peaks outside of the range were not considered.

Figure 7.30 shows the distribution of the market peaks between May 1st and July 31st for each year to identify what trends exist. These are not necessarily the absolute peak values for the year, but are the highest value for the timeframe.

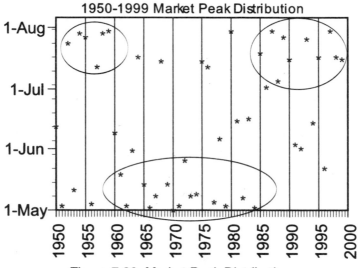

Figure 7.30: Market Peak Distribution

- In 17 cases (40% of the time) the peak value occurred in May. In 8 cases (16% of the time), the peak value occurred in June. July showed the highest number of peaks at 21 (or 44% of the time).

- The two concentrations of points signify that there are really **two distinct peaks**; one in early May and one around mid to late in July.

- We also noticed concentrations of points grouped by decades as circled above.

Average results by decade were examined to see if there was any pattern to the early or late peaks. To get a more accurate look at this period, May 1st was used as a starting point for ease of comparison. Figures 7.31 and 7.32 show the divergence in the peak patterns from decade to decade. This data illustrates that every decade will behave differently.

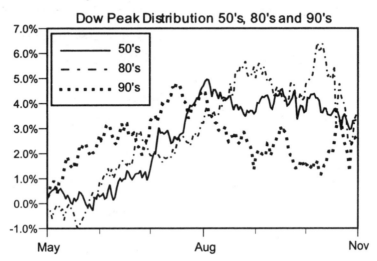

Figure 7.31 & 7.32: Distribution of the Dow Jones Index Peak

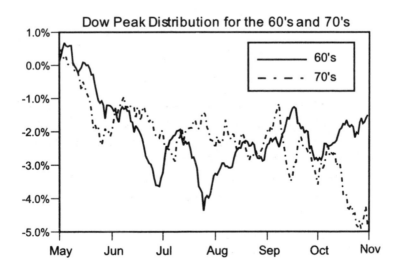

The results of the decade trend graphs and the scatter graph are consistent. While this data suggests that certain trends in peak values are influenced by market conditions, there is not enough evidence to derive a definite conclusion that enables us to incorporate these trends into our system. This peak distribution information suggests that perhaps bull markets like those seen in the 50's, 80's and 90's, tend to peak later in the year, specifically in July. At the same time, the data suggests that weaker markets like those seen in the 60's and 70's, tend to peak earlier in the year, specifically in May.

Selecting The Early Time Out Date

From the previous graphs, we knew that there must be a first peak in the market around the first of May. Each individual day, ranging from April 15th to May 31st was then examined using our model. This time, the Time In entry date of October 28th was used because it was already established as the superior entry date. Priority was given to finding a date that produced large returns along with limited downside risk.

We could justify sacrificing some return for a date that gave protection in the event of an early market pullback, that used to be so prevalent in the decades of the 1960's and 1970's. You may have heard the long-standing market saying: "Sell in May and Go Away". There is an element of truth in this.

Table 7.13 highlights the findings for dates ranging from April 15th to May 30th. These are based on long-term cumulative results from 1953 to 1999, using historic Dow index data.

There is a clear window of opportunity where the performance is higher than average. The average percentage return peaks at 9.88% on May 5th, which is much higher than the surrounding dates.

Please note that the abbreviations *TITO* and *TT* used in all of the following graphs and related appendices refer to the *Time In Time Out* system.

Table 7.13: Finding the First Time Out Date

Date	Return Ratio	Performance Ratio	Cumulative *TT* Market Return $	TT Average Ann Return %
15-Apr	114	242	4,354,258	9.09
20-Apr	119	247	4,560,374	9.22
25-Apr	120	241	4,690,766	9.31
01-May	131	255	5,172,837	9.55
05-May	**145**	**276**	**5,805,937**	**9.88**
10-May	129	240	5,205,302	9.63
15-May	134	244	5,636,847	9.71
20-May	122	216	4,850,635	9.52
25-May	105	182	4,044,899	9.16
30-May	117	199	4,534,233	9.43

From our analysis, May 5th was selected as the ideal early exit date for conservative investors, based on long-term performance.

Results for the Conservative Exit Date

This next section includes bar graphs that illustrate the results for the October 28th to May 5th Annual Cycle since 1953. The initial comparisons between our system and the Dow index, excludes dividends and interest. Subsequent comparisons include dividends and interest, along with total dollar gains. Following each graph, there is an explanation of the numbers and labels.

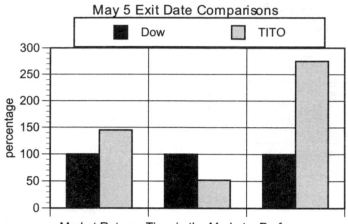

Figure 7.33: Comparing TITO Results to the Dow Index

What the Numbers Mean

- <u>Market Return</u> is the measurement by which our Annual Cycle outperformed the Dow on a buy and hold basis. May 5th showed excellent results at 145%. This means that the Annual Cycle produced 45% more return than the index by being selective about when to be in and out of the market.

- <u>Time in the Market</u> refers to how much of each year the *Time In Time Out* system calls for investment in the equity market. Here you can see that only 52% of the year is actually used, yet the system still beat the index by a good margin.

- <u>Performance Ratio</u> expresses how superior this system is when compared to buy and hold. Obtaining 145% of the Dow in only 52.4% of the year yields a reading of 276% performance; almost three times as efficient as buying and holding the index.

Comparisons Using Dividends and Interest

So far, the comparisons between *TITO* and buy and hold have been based solely on market returns. To ensure a complete comparison of the *Time In Time Out* system against the Dow index on a buy and hold basis, we added dividends and interest to the calculations.

The Dow Jones index earns dividends throughout the year which supplement the gain in value of the index. We obtained the actual amount of dividends produced each year for the Dow index from Barron's and included this data in our model. In doing so, we made it possible to accurately measure the full impact of these dividends on the total returns over any timeframe. This data has been included in the comparisons shown throughout the remainder of the book where indicated.

Time In Time Out earns dividends for the portion of the year when money is invested in the Dow index. When you are not invested in the Dow, interest is earned at the Federal Reserve discount rate. This is generally the same rate available to the average retail investor if they were buying short-term treasuries from a brokerage firm. Actual Federal Reserve historic data was added to the model for these calculations.

Figure 7.34 shows how the average annual percentage returns were measured in several different ways:

- Average % Return shows how much on average the Dow gained per year without dividends. On May 5th the result was 9.37% versus 9.88% for the *Time In Time Out* system, a difference of 0.51% per year. This may not seem like much of a difference, but imagine the effect if your money was to compound at a half a point higher rate of return every year for the rest of

your life. As you will see when we look at the total
dollars, it is a huge amount of money.

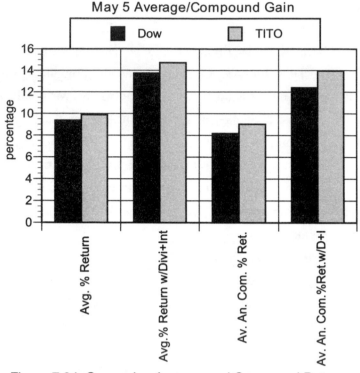

Figure 7.34: Comparing Average and Compound Returns

- Average % Return with Dividends and Interest shows a
  larger difference with a result of 13.74% for the Dow
  and 14.71% for the *Time In Time Out* system.
- Average Annual Compound % Return was prepared as
  a supplement for those investors wishing to make a
  comparison with mutual fund returns that are
  expressed in this format. Using this method of calculation produces a result of 8.17% for the Dow versus
  9.03% for our system in terms of market performance
  only.

- Average Annual Compound % Return with Dividends and Interest shows that with dividends and interest factored in, the results are 12.40% for the Dow versus 13.95% for our system. A 1.5% differential on a compounded basis is a major improvement from buying and holding.

Finally, every investor wants to know the bottom line: how much money they can make. The following comparison is based on an initial investment of $100,000 in 1953 to a final value in 1999.

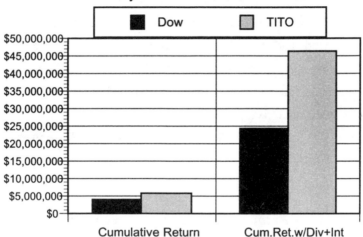

Figure 7.35: Total Dollar Returns on May 5th

The Total Dollars generated by market returns were $4.1 million for the index versus $5.8 million for our system. When all dividends and interest were factored in that total rose to $24.34 million for the Dow versus $46.34 million for our system.

Appendix A: Conservative Time In Exit Date details the findings for the May 5th exit date for all years. The numbers are presented on a cumulative basis to show the long-term benefit of a repetitive plan. The results for each individual year can be measured by reading the data on the "sell" line. Refer to this appendix if you would like to see a full listing of returns produced since 1953.

Other advantages of May 5th as an exit

Other dates that emerged from the analysis provided a higher rate of market return, so why was May 5th the optimum date for conservative investors? The answer is that market performance could not be the sole criteria used in the selection process. Other factors were also considered such as downside risk, interest earning potential, and relative performance of the model against the market. To conservative investors, these are important considerations.

In Figure 7.30, you saw how the peaks varied during the May to July period, and we suggested that a conservative investor may want to select the May 5th exit date. Table 7.13 showed how cumulative returns declined after reaching a peak on May 5th. We concluded that the additional risk produced by staying in the market beyond May 5th is not worth any additional potential gain, for conservative investors. Think of May 5th as the date that allows you to <u>sell into the strength</u> of the market and earn more interest on your cash.

How Frequently has this strategy worked?

As shown in **Appendix A: Conservative Time In Exit Date**, 38 out of 46 cycles have provided positive returns with this strategy. **This is 83% of the time**. In fact, 1984 was the last time that our strategy did not produce a positive return.

The remaining eight cycles were not successful because they occurred during unstable economic periods, such as the recession in 1974. During years like this one, a buy and hold strategy would lose more money than the *Time In Time Out* strategy.

We do not suggest that this system outperforms the Dow every year because there are times when the market does not decline in the summer months, but instead keeps advancing right through to the end of the year. The year 1996 is a perfect example of this effect, since some gains were missed. The real objective is to have a system that beats the market over the long run by being repetitive, and avoids the declines in those years where the market pulls back sharply. How we do this is described in the **Analyzing the Time Out Cycles** section.

According to our market research, most investors reading this book would probably find the conservative approach a good fit with their objectives. Conservative investors like the idea of having a plan with less risk and less stress, as much as the idea of better returns.

Determining the Aggressive Time Out Date

Depending on your objectives, there are good arguments for using a later exit date. Not every investor wants to be a conservative investor, and so these investors can use the second approach we have developed.

If you are younger, you may want your capital to grow more than you want to protect it. This is why financial planners always encourage people in their 20's and 30's to be more heavily weighted in equities. While stocks offer greater returns in the long run, they are more volatile in the short-term. The more years that you have for your planning horizon, the more risk you can tolerate. This is financial common sense but worth repeating these days, with some people approaching retirement and taking excessive risk with their money.

Another reason why you may want to consider a later exit date is to maximize your return with only a portion of your capital.

Typically, an investor considering this later exit date has money invested elsewhere that is providing some security like a bond, GIC, annuity, a rental property, etc. They are only concerned about getting the most out of the dollars they commit to the equity market rather than security.

If either of these scenarios apply to you, then consider delaying your exit until the second peak, occurring later in July. Looking back at Figure 7.29, the 5 and 15 year averages show the peak occurring at this later date, more so than the 45 year average. This graph shows the benefit of delaying your exit date. We went through the same procedure of testing the July exit as previously done for the May exit. The highlights are shown in Table 7.14.

Table 7.14: Finding the Late Exit Date

Date	Return Ratio	Performance Ratio	*TT* Market Return %	*TT* Average Return %
July 1	139	204	5,623,439	10.14
July 5	156	226	6,341,331	10.44
July 10	181	257	7,395,706	10.81
July 15	191	266	7,824,550	10.92
July 19	**198**	**271**	**8,086,776**	**10.98**
July 25	177	237	7,686,243	10.85
July 30	177	237	7,050,244	10.69

- The return ratio climbed dramatically over a few days between July 15th and 20th, so it was clear there was a market top.
- Generally, the returns were higher on these days than the earlier exit date in May.

We found the best results occurred on **July 19th**. **This is your sell date.** For full results on how the July 19th exit date has performed since 1953, please refer to **Appendix B: Aggressive Time In Exit Date**.

Results for the Aggressive Exit Date

July 19th produced some extraordinary results, considering it is only 75 days past May 5th. Using an initial investment of $100,000 in 1953, resulted in $8,086,776 total dollar returns by exiting on July 19th each year, until 1999. This compares with a return of $4,093,560 for the Dow. That is an astounding **198%** of index value and a large increase from the 145% return of May 5th. This is an exceptional "Double The Dow" strategy.

Using *Time In Time Out*, conservative and aggressive investors have both been able to substantially outperform the Dow index since 1953. Table 7.15 shows a summary of the performance differential between the May 5th and July 19th exit dates. In both cases *they are compared with the Dow on a buy and hold basis.*

Table 7.15: Total Dollar Comparison for Dow index and TITO

Indicator	May 5 Exit	July 19 Exit
Dow return dollars	$4,008,562	$4,093,560
TITO dollars	**$5,805,937**	**$8,086,775**
Dow dollars with dividends	$24,340,000	$23,990,000
TITO w/ dividends+interest	**$46,340,000**	**$55,170,000**
Average Dow % return	9.37%	9.52%
Average TITO % return	**9.88%**	**10.97%**
Avg. Dow % ret. With/div.	13.74%	13.78%
Avg. TITO% with div+int.	**14.71%**	**15.51%**

- **TITO dollars** illustrate the large performance differential of the market return from May 5th to July 19th. The 1.1% average index increase has compounded into millions of dollars, almost 30% more.
- **TITO with dividends and interest** shows that 20% more return was achieved by the later exit date.

The following graphs illustrate the difference in performance between exit dates. Figure 7.36 illustrates the dollar comparison for the May 5th and July 19th exit dates. The *Dow* columns represent the index return for buy and hold. The *TITO* columns represent the effect of buying and selling each year at the same times. Regardless of which exit date you choose, *Time In Time Out* generates more return than buy and hold.

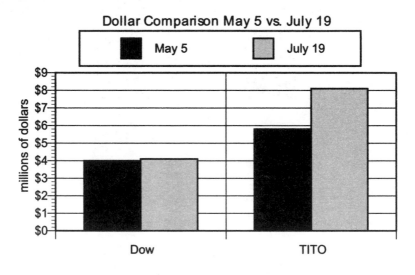

Figure 7.36: Dollar Comparison of Exit Dates

Figure 7.37 compares total dollar returns, including dividends and interest. As in the previous graph, the *Dow with dividends* represents the index return for buy and hold, while the *TITO with dividends and interest*, represents the results of using *Time In Time Out*.

The effect of adding dividends and interest to the market returns substantially increases the performance of both the *Time In Time Out* and the Dow buy and hold strategies. It is interesting that the relative performance of our system to the Dow increases with the inclusion of dividends and interest.

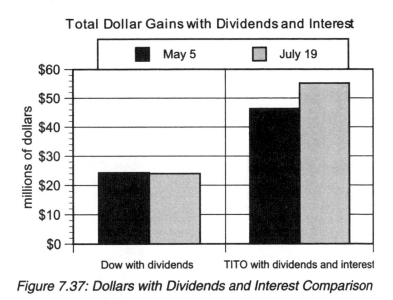

Figure 7.37: Dollars with Dividends and Interest Comparison

Figure 7.38 shows average annual returns per year. The *Dow* represents the average return of the Dow index for buy and hold, while *TITO* represents the average *Time In Time Out* return.

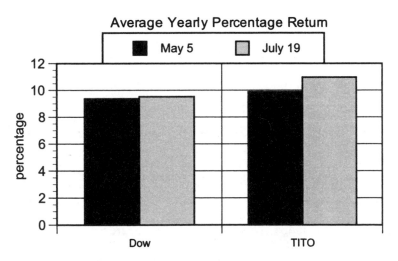

Figure 7.38: Average Annual Return for Exit Dates

Figure 7.39 also shows average annual returns, only now all of the dividends and interest have been added and reinvested.

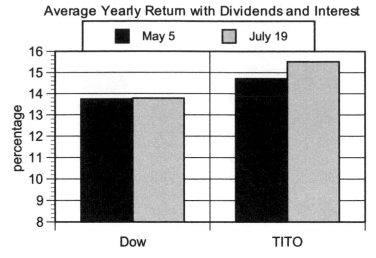

Figure 7.39: Average Annual Return with reinvested income

How Has The S&P500 Performed with this System?

Earlier in this chapter, Figure 7.28 compared the Dow and the S&P500 for the past fifty years. The index trends were almost identical, but the S&P500 had the overall advantage in terms of performance. Since the S&P500 is a much broader index, the larger number of stocks tend to reduce the volatility somewhat, so that it does not display the same degree of seasonality as the Dow.

For the period of 1953 to 1999 shown in Table 7.16, the conservative exit date of May 5th for the Annual Cycle could not beat the S&P500 index in terms of market return. However, our system beat the S&P500 by approximately 30% in total dollars, with dividends and interest included. This is not the same degree of superior performance seen when comparing against the Dow, but our system still offers a substantial increase in the total benefit to investors.

When using the July 19th date, *Time In Time Out* produced much higher returns and came close to doubling the S&P500 index with dividends and interest added. Investors who have difficulty using the Dow for any reason will also benefit greatly from using our system with the S&P500 index.

Table 7.16: Comparing Exit Dates with the S&P500 Index

Indicator	May 5 Exit	July 19 Exit
S&P500 return dollars	$5,553,627	$5,802,350
TITO **dollars**	**$4,997,621**	**$8,581,307**
S&P500 $ with dividends	$27,940,000	$28,480,000
TITO **$ with div+int**	**$36,560,000**	**$51,830,000**
Average S&P500 % return	10.04%	10.39%
Avg. *TITO* % return	**9.51%**	**11.17%**
Avg. S&P500 % ret. w/div	14.17%	14.27%
Avg. *TITO* % ret. w/div+int.	**14.16%**	**15.47%**

Does Nasdaq also follow the same patterns?

In recent years it seems that the Nasdaq exchange has advanced during the whole year, showing little signs of a pullback during the summer months. However, when the Nasdaq data from 1985 to 1999 was tested, *Time In Time Out* was able to produce a very large improvement on returns, as shown by Table 7.17.

Table 7.17: Comparing Exit Dates with the Nasdaq Index

Indicator	May 5 Exit	July 19 Exit
Nasdaq return dollars	$807,622	$977,764
TITO dollars	**$804,465**	**$1,614,745**
Average Nasdaq % return	16.14%	19.25%
Avg. TITO % return	**16.45%**	**23.25%**

For Canadian Readers

The *Time In Time Out* system was also verified using the Canadian TSE300 data to ensure consistency, but there were a few limitations. Historic data was available only from 1985 to 1999 without dividends, so the results shown are limited to market returns and average percentage return for a 15-year period. We found that our system is extremely effective as it almost doubled the index return in a short 15-year period. In fact, these results are some of the best we have found with our system in terms of adding value over buy and hold, regardless of the exit date.

Table 7.18: Comparing Exit Dates with the TSE300 Index

Indicator	May 5 Exit	July 19 Exit
TSE300 return dollars	$266,752	$276,334
Time In Time Out **dollars**	**$358,525**	**$523,833**
Average TSE300 % return	7.87%	8.23%
Avg. TITO % return	**10.01%**	**12.99%**

Success of Time In Time Out in the 1990's

There was concern that the results would be different for the 1990's, given the strength of the bull market and the weakness in interest rates. Would the *Time In Time Out* system hold up as well as it had since 1953 with these two factors at work? In previous decades, the opposite of these two elements (i.e. average markets with high interest rates) were positive contributors to the success of our system in outperforming the index. To find our answer, we ran the model program for the ten year period of the 1990's.

The following table demonstrates the effect of both the conservative and aggressive exit strategies, covering only the 1990 to 1999 period. It is true that the margin of superiority has not been as great in the past ten years compared with the long-term results, but the aggressive approach shows the most improvement.

Table 7.19: Comparing Exit Date Returns for the last 10 Years

Indicator	May 5 Exit	July 19 Exit
Dow return dollars only	$449,710	$459,246
TITO **dollars only**	**$377,146**	**$480,385**
Dow dollars, with dividends	$557,649	$567,364
TITO **dollars with dividends and interest**	**$498,801**	**$614,723**
Average Dow % return	17.75%	18.29%
Average *TITO* % return	**16.25%**	**19.51%**
Average Dow % return with dividends	20.68%	21.12%
Average *TITO* % with dividends and interest.	**16.88%**	**22.41%**
Average Dow Compound return	16.22%	16.46%
Average *TITO* Compound return	**14.19%**	**16.99%**
Average Dow Compounded with dividends	18.75%	18.95%
Average *TITO* Compounded with div and int	**17.43%**	**19.91%**

- *Time In Time Out* has missed matching the returns of buying and holding the Dow, with a May 5th exit date over the past ten years. In the face of the strongest bull market and some of the lowest interest rates in history, it is a great accomplishment to achieve 90% of the total dollar gains.

- With strong markets comes volatility. The *Time In Time Out* system has managed to miss most of the declines and still managed to beat the index by an average of 1.2% using the July exit date.

- The average annual compound rate of return was a full 1% higher than the Dow with dividends and interest factored in.

- A late exit date works better with a strong bull market.

Analyzing the Time Out Cycles

So far we have been showing all of the positive benefits of being in the market at particular times, and the excellent results generated by following the Time In portion of the Annual Cycle.

Now let us examine the results for the Dow during the Time Out period; *when you should be out of the market.* Earlier in this chapter, we showed the period in the summer when prices began falling and volatility began increasing. Figure 7.40 enlarges this timeframe, which we call the Time Out period for conservative investors. The graph illustrates the average Dow index movements from 1953 to 1999. The 10, 25 and 46 year patterns from May 6th to October 27th are examined in this graph.

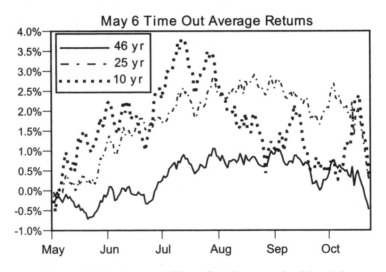

Figure 7.40: Average Time Out Returns for May 6th

Notice how the market has changed very little from May 6th to October 27th by each trendline ending close to a 0% change.

<u>*Actual results:*</u>
10-year = 0.40 %
25-year = 0.29 %
46-year = -0.48 %

What does this mean in dollars?

Appendix C: Conservative Time Out Period details the results for the Dow index during the Time Out period of May 6th to October 27th. The numbers are presented on a cumulative basis to show the long-term erosion of capital from 1953 to 1999.

We found that investing in the Time Out period would have produced a cumulative loss of 36%! If you invested $100,000 into the Dow index on May 6th and sold on October 27th each year from 1953 to 1999, you would have had absolutely no gain. In fact, your $100,000 would be worth $64,356. No one would consciously do this, but in effect, it happens to buy and hold investors. Their money declines with the market during the Time Out period.

You would think that over the course of 46 years there would be some gain made in the summer time, since the financial industry states that the market always increases over the long-term. After all, participating in the market for 48% of the year from May 6th to October 27th leads to expectations of earning something!

History has shown that this is not the case. The Time Out period is a terrible time to be invested. The 36% cumulative result from above equals an average annual percentage return of -0.49%, with losses 22 of those 46 years. *The market actually went down 48% of the time and some of the declines were substantial.* History dispels the myth that the market only increases over time!

Does July 20th to October 27th produce better results?

The answer to this question is **no**. As a matter of fact, the results for this period are quite harsh.

The following graph shows the 10, 25 and 46 year averages for the July 20th to October 27th Time Out period from 1953 to 1999, with the July 20th values reset to zero for accurate comparison. Note this time how all the averages are negative at the end of each trendline.

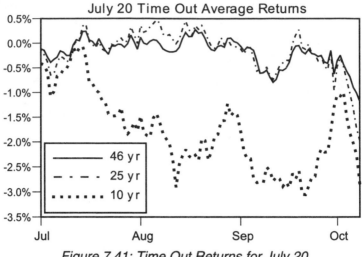

Figure 7.41: Time Out Returns for July 20

Actual results:
10 yr = -2.84 %
25 yr = -1.98 %
46 yr = -1.18 %

Appendix D: Aggressive Time Out Period details the effect of investing in the market during this Time Out period of July 20th to October 27th.

This time, there would have been a loss of 53% of the original capital, meaning that the $100,000 initial investment would have shrunk to $47,415. This is an average return of -1.18% per year for 46 years! How could this time period be so bad?

The answer lies in several key factors:

1. This timeframe has seen declines in 24 of the 46 years (or 52% of the time). Some of the worse declines, corrections, and even crashes have occurred in the months from July to October. When you look at the list of poor performing

months, May, August, September and even October are among the worst of the year. A look at Table 7.20 also shows that some of the worst days of market performance in the last five decades have happened during the Time Out period.

Table 7.20: The Worst Days of the Time Out Period Since 1953

Day 1	Day 2	Day 3	Day 4	Day 5
10/19/87	10/26/87	10/27/97	10/13/89	9/26/55
-22.61%	-8.04%	-7.18%	-6.90%	-6.54%
Day 6	Day 7	Day 8	Day 9	Day 10
8/31/98	9/11/86	10/16/87	8/27/98	10/22/87
-6.37%	-4.61%	-4.60%	-4.19%	-3.82%

2. In the past ten years (1990 to 1999) the market has declined severely five out of ten times from July 20th to October 27th. If this is happening during the greatest bull market in history, does it not make sense that there is an established pattern involved?

3. Anytime you are investing in a period that shows the severity of declines like this period has, you need some big gains to just break even. Since 1953, seventeen declines were in the 0%-10% range, six were in the 10%-20% range, and one was over 20%. Avoiding these declines is a priority of the *TITO* system, and a major factor to its success.

Best and Worst Market days: Dow Jones 1990-1999

Appendix E: The Best and Worst Days details the best and worst performing days that have occurred over the previous ten years.

Caveats on Using July 19th as an exit date for Time In

If you have the ability to withstand more risk, and are purely focusing on market return, July 19th is the day to choose. Here are some things to be aware of, however:

- Although the market exhibits a 44% probability of peaking in July, it is impossible to tell exactly when the market will peak in any given year. If it peaks early, the value would be lower when you exit in July.

- Recent years have experienced more late peaks which boost the results. This pattern may not hold, as it could reverse to a pattern of early peaks as in previous decades.

- Interest rates may go back up to levels that will make the conservative date of May 5th look better again in the future. The compounding of interest may exceed the market gains made with a later exit date.

Final notes about the Time Out Cycle

- You will earn more in the long run by staying out of the market from May or July through to October.
- Keep your capital safe and earning interest by staying in cash or money market during the Time Out period.

Examining the Individual Months of the Year

The explanation of the Annual Cycle would not be complete without looking at the individual months of the year. This is done to give you an overview of how the market moves throughout the year and to reinforce the merits of our system by examining its components.

Starting with what we call the first month, November, look at the progress made during the first six months. Figure 7.42 shows the typical monthly movements using the long-term average percent gains from 1953 to 1999.

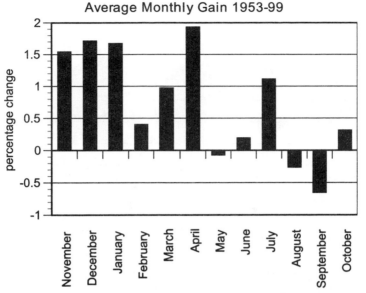

Figure 7.42: Average monthly gain from 1953 - 1999

Table 7.21 ranks the months in order of average percentage gain since 1953 to the end of 1999, and also shows the percentage of times the month has produced a positive return. This data explains much of the success of *Time In Time Out*.

Whether the conservative or aggressive approach is selected, the top four performing months historically are included in the Time In period (April, December, January, and November). Also included are March and February, the sixth and seventh best months respectively. Aggressive investors also derive benefit from the fifth best month, which is July.

In addition to the average gains, it is also important to understand that the probability of positive performance is very high for the top months. All of them exhibit a 60% or better chance of gain, except for February which is at 57%.

Table 7.21: Ranking Monthly Gains since 1953

Month	Average Gain %	% of Time as positive Month	Return Rank
November	1.54	67	4
December	1.71	70	2
January	1.67	67	3
February	0.40	57	7
March	0.97	63	6
April	1.93	63	1
May	-0.07	50	10
June	0.19	54	9
July	1.11	57	5
August	-0.26	57	11
September	-0.65	35	12
October	0.31	59	8

Now compare the months making up the Time Out period. If you are following the conservative strategy, you will be out of the market during the May to October period, when there have been negative results in the months of May, August and September. Aggressive investors do not avoid the negative influence of May, but make off-setting gains in June and July. During the Time Out period, buy and hold investors have had no choice but to watch helplessly as their profits erode.

Monthly Historical Data

The next set of graphs illustrate the movements of the markets during all months of the year, based on average data from 1953 to 1999. The purpose of these graphs is to show the movements that occur in each month, whether positive or negative, as well as the degree of volatility. **Appendix F: Dow Jones Index Monthly Gains** outlines the full returns for each month and each year, dating back to 1953.

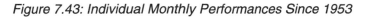
Figure 7.43: Individual Monthly Performances Since 1953

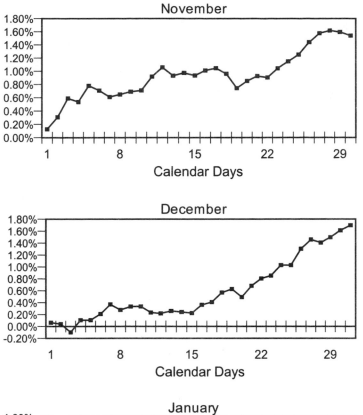

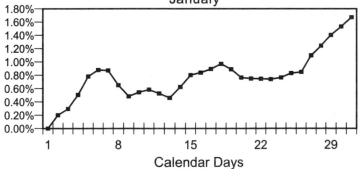

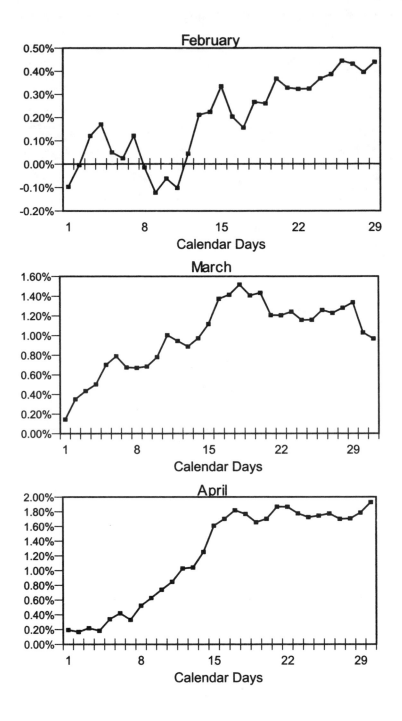

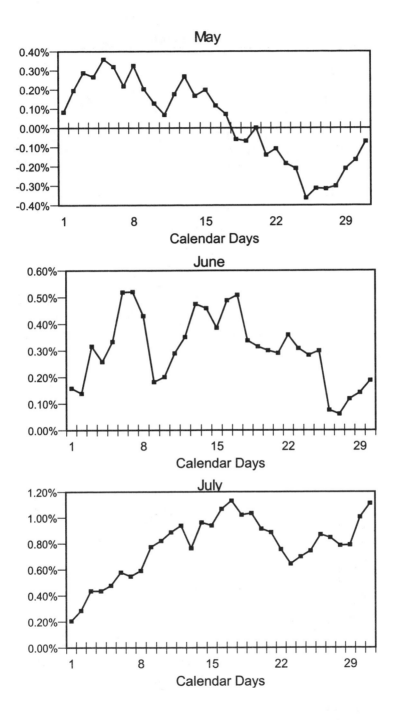

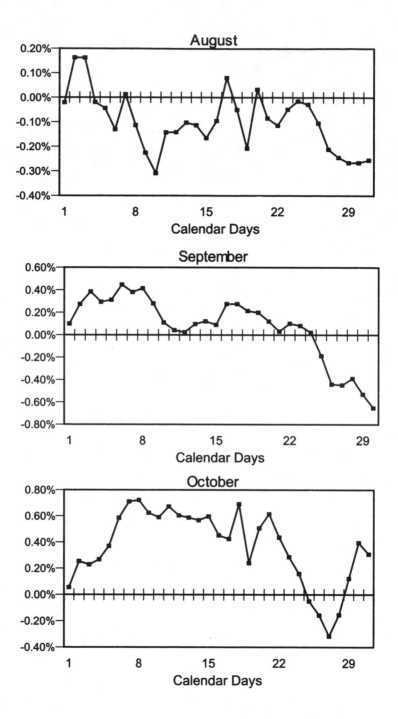

The Tools You Need

Now that you understand the exact entry and exit dates for the Annual Cycle and you have decided either to take the conservative or aggressive approach, a discussion of the required tools is in order. This section will make the execution of the plan much easier.

You must decide the type of account to have for your particular needs and the specific investments to use for successful implementation of the *Time In Time Out* system. Fundamentally, it is quite easy and straightforward to start using the system, but there are options to consider for the implementation which carry varying degrees of complexity.

For example, if you are a diehard mutual fund fan, you may want a way to incorporate the principles of the *Time In Time Out* system using funds in order to stay within your comfort level. The same concept holds true for a dedicated stock trader who believes in the system equally, but prefers to use stocks as the vehicle. If you are starting with cash, you may want some guidelines on setting up your portfolio.

Regardless of your style or previous investment experience, there is an ideal solution that will suit your needs and be very cost effective. We will outline several different methods to choose from, which will all deliver excellent results. The decision really comes down to your preferences or beliefs regarding the products.

For Mutual Fund Investors

If you are in this group, you have a wealth of options available. There are now thousands of *actively managed funds* to choose from, as well as hundreds of *passively managed index funds* to consider. For those who may not be familiar with these terms, an actively managed fund is one where the manager attempts to select stocks that they feel will be outstanding performers. These are then bought and sold according to how the manager views the prospects for the stock or the market in general. Index funds are passive in the sense that the manager holds all the stocks that make up a market index in the same proportion to the index weighting. The stocks are then held without change unless the index changes.

Actively managed funds have been a part of any investor's mutual fund portfolio for a long time, especially for those investors seeking access to certain foreign markets or special sectors of the economy such as technology, small companies, or bio-tech. Regardless of the actively managed funds' objective, the same problem exists: namely, they are *always* invested. This of course is contrary to what the *Time In Time Out* system mandates.

The best way to handle this obstacle from our experience, is to stay with a family of actively managed funds that permit no-cost switches throughout the year. That way you can elect to move in and out of the market at anytime without incurring switch fees or penalties. You could then buy the equity funds in October and sell them in May or July, switching to a money market fund until October when the cycle starts over. Check with your mutual fund provider before entering orders because the policies of fund companies vary widely regarding switch fees.

The easiest way to implement calendar investing over the long-term is to use passively managed index funds in lieu of actively managed funds wherever possible. Flexibility and cost are two of the obvious reasons for this, but the fundamental argument is really performance. Earlier it was explained that only 11% of actively managed funds can beat their benchmark index, and those indices keep changing constantly. Given these conditions, it makes far more sense to use an index product that will give you at least the benchmark level of return. Then, using the *Time In Time Out* strategy will provide the extra level of performance that enables you to beat the index.

Regardless of where you buy your funds now (a bank, trust, mutual fund company, or a brokerage), they probably have some index products to choose from. The problem often found is that there are few places where the entire selection of funds is made available in one portfolio. For example, a fund account at your bank may be limited to holding just their own proprietary fund products, and they may not have a full line of index funds. The same holds true if you are dealing with a fund company directly. They will only offer their own funds, limiting you in scope.

In theory, the average investor only needs four basic types of index funds to get started with a passive portfolio containing all asset classes:

- A Dow Jones 30 or S&P500 index fund for domestic equity exposure
- An International index fund for foreign equity exposure
- A fixed-income index fund for bond market exposure
- A money market fund for cash exposure.

As you will see in Chapter 9, **Build Your Own Portfolio**, if you have these basic funds available where you invest now then you have everything you need to get started. If not, you will need to check out some other companies with which to do business. While we try to stay impartial, links to some excellent websites and companies have been provided in this chapter to assist in your search. The more products you have to choose from, the more you can diversify and customize your portfolio.

For Self-Directed Investors Using Discount Brokers

If you are currently dealing with a *discount brokerage service*, or plan to in the future, the task of converting to a passive strategy will be made even easier. This is because discount services offer a greater range of products to choose from, including index mutual funds from most fund companies, and the relatively new but growing line of ETF's (exchange traded funds). A greater selection of products provides you with the ability to mirror almost any index in the world, and all of your holdings will show on a single account statement. This is a convenient and inexpensive solution. Some of the discount brokerage firms have even created their own index mutual funds because they recognize the tremendous ground-swell of interest in these products.

Exchange traded funds are baskets of securities that make up the various indices such as the S&P500, The Dow Jones Industrial Index, Nasdaq Composite and the Russell2000. They trade the same way as individual stocks, and at the same low commission rates offered by your brokerage firm. These ETF's are revolutionizing the way people invest, and they happen to be perfect for use with our calendar investing strategy.

For those of you using a Full-Service Broker

Investors will probably not abandon stockpicking completely for index investing anytime soon, due to their long-standing belief in owning select companies. As a result, there will always be the need for full-service brokers to help clients build and maintain a portfolio in partnership. Good brokers continue to attract their fair share of the market despite the rise of do-it-yourself investing.

If you have a good relationship with a broker, you will likely not want to change your way of doing business completely. Perhaps however, there is room in your plan for using an index strategy with a portion of your capital. If you find that you are not achieving the returns of the indices lately and want to ensure you do not fall behind in performance, indexing is a great solution. In this case, your broker can help you select some of the ETF's which trade like stocks, in lieu of some of the weaker performing holdings you may have now.

If you ask your broker about market seasonality, chances are that they have observed it themselves to a degree, or at least read about it. There is also a good possibility that they have lived through several of the major downturns that have occurred in the past, and therefore they would be more than happy to learn about ways to avoid declines. This book would be a welcome addition to your broker's research library, and can assist both of you to develop profitable strategies that take advantage of price and volatility trends.

The Benefits of Index Products

Regardless of where you have decided to hold your account, you need to know more about which products to buy and sell when it comes to implementing the strategy. So far, we have mentioned the Dow Jones Industrial Average (or Dow Jones index) almost exclusively, with some minor references to other indices. This is due to the strength of the Dow as a performance benchmark combined with the importance of the companies contained in it. Our suggestion is to stick with the Dow whenever possible unless you wish to concentrate more specifically on the broader market by using the S&P500.

Reasons to Love The Dow Index

- All of our historical data and patterns use the Dow Jones index as the underlying data source. The Dow exhibits more volatility than the broader market, so calendar investing produces a greater performance advantage.

- The index contains some of the best companies in the world with proven track records of earnings and profitability. Does anyone think they can find many investments superior to these?

- The Dow is dynamic and will change with the times to keep a portfolio of stocks representative of the modern economy.

Some Good Reasons to Index

When you examine the options available for implementation of the *Time In Time Out* strategy, certain styles make more sense than others. For instance, would you consider it wise or cost-effective to buy twelve blue-chip stocks on October 28th each year paying full commissions, then turn around on May 5th and sell them? We do not think that many investors would view this as a practical method because of the cost involved, and the difficult challenge of picking the twelve best stocks for your portfolio out of a universe of thousands.

It would probably be easier for most people to use a vehicle that incorporates a broader cross-section of the market, like the index products we discuss and pay just one commission.

Individual stock selection brings more challenge and pitfalls to the investor than just buying the index. If only 11% of all professional money managers match or beat the index over time, why should anyone think they could do better? Furthermore, Barclay's

Global Investors produced a study showing that the average U.S. large-cap stock manager (large cap meaning the same stocks as the Dow or S&P500 components) underperformed the market index by 0.5% over the period of 1987 to 1997. This does not seem like much but consider that $100,000 earning 0.5% more each year yields another $500 in your pocket each year. With compounding, this seemingly small difference can snowball into a huge dollar amount over time.

Consider that same $100,000 portfolio over 20 years, using a 10% rate of return versus a 10.5% rate of return.

- at 10% it grows to $672,749
- at 10.5% it grows to $736,623

Ted Cadsby, in his book *The Power of Index Funds*, compared the performance of U.S. active large-cap stock fund managers against the S&P500 index and subtracted 0.9% of the index returns to simulate the fees associated with the typical index fund. Over the last ten years, he found that none of those managers were able to beat the index on this basis! The same result was found for European Equity fund managers as well. The situation was better for Canadian managers, where 44% of them managed to outperform the TSE300 index.

Why is it that most actively managed funds cannot match or beat the index? There are several factors at work:

- First, they have much higher management fees in order to pay the brokers and maintain a large staff of analysts. This even happens even with no-load funds.
- Second, the trading costs are higher because turnover in actively managed funds is much greater as the manager adjusts the portfolio.

- Third, there is typically more cost incurred to market the fund. Some estimates range as high as a 2% penalty that active managers have to overcome just to match their passive management counterparts. For a large portfolio, that it is a huge difference to make up.

Indexing is inexpensive because management fees are very low and commissions are kept to a minimum due to the buy and hold nature of the index. Therefore, more of the gains will end up in your pocket at retirement. This alone could increase your rate of return by over 2% per year according to some studies.

If you own a fund that has outperformed the index by a wide margin, by all means stick with it. You should however, make sure you have the ability to get in and get out without incurring fees. This will allow you to use the *Time In Time Out* system and keep more of your profits. Also, check to make sure there are no commission charges. If you look at a graph of that fund's performance, it has likely fluctuated in a similar fashion to the market index throughout the years. Using calendar investing techniques can boost your returns.

For all of these reasons, it makes sense that the index strategy is the preferable course. This is especially true when you consider that most index funds are no-load, which means there is no cost incurred when you buy them and sell them. This may not be true with all institutions, so we suggest checking with them first. In most cases however, the use of index funds is ideal for implementing the *Time In Time Out* system.

It appears many investors agree with us on the benefits of indexing because recent figures indicate that in 1999, roughly 50% of all mutual fund deposits in the U.S. went into index funds.

Index Mutual Funds

Presently, there are over 100 index mutual funds available for purchase and that number keeps increasing daily. Despite the growing popularity, index investing is so low key (and low cost) that many companies do not advertise their products much, so it is a challenge to find them all.

Some of the best sources of information are on the internet, and are surprisingly unbiased. For example, www.indexfunds.com is a terrific website that contains information on over 180 index products (some of which are ETF's) as well as articles and news pertaining to index investing. All of the major index families are represented such as Vanguard, Dreyfus, Schwab, Fidelity, etc. The listings also include the loads and total annual fees. This makes the selection process very easy for the average investor. Of course you should check the performance of the funds that interest you and examine their prospectus for all the details.

Another good source for news and articles dealing with index investing and associated performance can be found at the following address: www.mutualfunds.about.com. They have a wealth of articles on the subject.

Then of course there are the websites of fund companies themselves, including the discount brokers who have launched their own funds. These are more useful for product listings and performance numbers but they should be reviewed:

- www.vanguard.com
- www.etrade.com
- www.schwab.com
- www.tdwaterhouse.com

Most of the index funds you find in the listings on these sites deal with the S&P500 index, rather than the Dow. Until recently, there was little interest in building a product to mirror the Dow index. With the increase in self-directed investment and the growth of the discount brokerage business, it is not surprising to find these firms on the leading edge of the trend to provide an investment vehicle for the Dow.

A specific mention goes to TD Waterhouse with their no-load Dow 30 fund, launched recently as a result of strong demand. More information on this fund can be found on their website.

What if I cannot find a Dow index fund?

The alternative would be to use an index mutual fund that mirrors the S&P500 index, and there are many of them available. There are a few reasons for the lack of Dow funds that we observe:

- Indexing is a recent trend that seems to be just now getting the full attention of the individual investor. Prior to 1998 there was little demand for these products, so few existed. For example, Diamonds (DIA, an ETF) was conceived in 1998.

- It is very difficult to spread billions of dollars among just 30 stocks without taking control positions in those companies, so most really large index managers and pension plan trustees prefer to have more selection available to them. Therefore, the trend is to use the S&P500 index as a base where there is a lot more opportunity for diversification.

- There was more interest in the S&P500 than in the Dow up until the past few years. The Dow index did not contain many resource, technology or life science companies; sectors of the economy that have been growing at a great pace. Recent inclusions of such companies as Microsoft and Intel in the Dow index have changed this perception and made the Dow much more attractive to investors. The investment industry is responding by creating new Dow-based products as quickly as they can.

There are only minor performance differences in the Dow and S&P500 indices over the long-term so your returns should not be vastly different, and from our analysis neither should the seasonal patterns. It is true that there are occasions where the Dow jumps ahead of the broader index for a period of time (or vice versa) but over several business cycles this difference will not be significant. For example, the five year performance numbers for each index as of December 31, 1999 are:

- Dow = 27.1%
- S&P500 = 28.7%

If you are not able to use a Dow index product for whatever reason, using products based on the S&P500 index is a perfectly acceptable alternative; your returns will not be dramatically different.

Index Mutual Funds for Canadian Readers

In Canada there are several companies who have entered the index fund foray in a big way during 1999. While there are nowhere near the number of funds available in Canada as there are in the U.S., the rapid growth in this area suggests that indexing may become a large sector of the mutual fund industry in a few short years.

Two companies stand out in this field. The first is TD Greenline, which is the fund division of TD bank (the parent company of TD Waterhouse brokerage). They have launched a series of 11 index funds that cover the domestic Canadian index (the TSE300) as well as the major U.S. and International markets. The good news for Canadians is that indexing also works well to provide eligibility for Registered Retirement Savings Plans which are subject to foreign content. More information can be found on the bank's website at www.tdbank.ca.

The other company making great strides in the index fund arena is Canadian Imperial Bank of Commerce (CIBC). Their mutual fund division has launched a series of 12 index funds, covering a variety of markets, and many of them are eligible for RRSP's while being diversified internationally. Ted Casday heads up CIBC's mutual fund division, and he has just written a book entitled *The Power of Index Funds* which you may find interesting. More information on these index funds can be found on their website at www.cibc.com.

Exchange Traded Funds (or ETF's)

The really big story of the last few years, and perhaps into the next few, has been the explosive growth of exchange-traded funds. These products are not the *open-ended mutual funds* that you may be familiar with; they are actually *closed-ended investment trusts* that trade like stocks on the Amex (American Stock Exchange).

Closed-ended ETF's have a limited number of shares outstanding so that new money is not flowing in all of the time. Similarly, redemptions (or cash outflows) are not occurring all of the time. This simplifies the task of managing these funds and results in lower management fees.

Amex pioneered this investment innovation several years ago when it introduced the first ETF called SPDR's (Standard and Poors Depository Receipts). It took a while for this product to become popular with investors as it was a totally new concept, but with the launch of QQQ's (Nasdaq tracking stock) and Diamond's (Dow Jones Industrial Average index units), these index products became a mainstay of the stock market and many investors' portfolios.

Today, there are over fifty Index Shares available for trading on the Amex exchange covering a broad range of market indices and sectors of the economy. Regardless of the names they go by, they all have one thing in common: they allow you to buy or sell shares of an entire portfolio of stocks in a single security.

Benefits of Index Shares.

For a small investor, instant diversification alone is enough to justify the use of index shares, but there are additional advantages:

- Index shares can be bought or sold anytime throughout the trading day at the prevailing market price. This is a major advantage over open-ended mutual funds that are transacted at the end of the day and priced on the closing index level. There is no guess-work associated with your transaction price.
- Index shares incur very low management fees, usually 0.15% to 0.5% depending on the manager. This is approximately 1.0% to 1.5% lower than a typical actively-managed mutual fund, and the difference stays in the investor's pocket.
- Index shares trade on the same commission schedule as a stock
- Index shares are eligible for margin in your taxable trading account.
- Index funds pay out dividends to shareholders if they are earned in the fund.

- Index shares are tax efficient due to the lack of capital gains being triggered by the fund manager. It should be noted that this may or may not be the case going forward and the potential for taxable capital gains to be generated does exist.

With all these great features and benefits, it is understandable why index shares are becoming so popular, and increasing in number and asset size every month.

Diamonds

Armed with all this information on index shares, our suggested investment vehicle for use with the *Time In Time Out* system is "Diamonds Trust", or better known as "Diamonds". This is a closed end trust that contains the 30 stocks making up the Dow Jones Industrial Average. Diamonds trade on the Amex exchange under the symbol "DIA".

More information on the trust units can be easily found by going to the Amex website (www.amex.com) and requesting information under the symbol "DIA".

DIAMONDS Trust Series 1
Schedule of Investments
October 31, 1999

Table 8.22: Schedule of Investments for Diamonds Trust Series

Common Stocks	Shares	Value
Alcoa, Inc.	472,587	$ 28,709,660
Allied Signal Inc.	472,587	$ 26,907,922
American ExpressCo.	472,587	$ 72,778,398
A T & T Corp.	472,587	$ 22,093,442
Boeing Co.	472,587	$ 21,768,539
Caterpillar, Inc.	472,587	$ 26,110,432
Citigroup, Inc.	472,587	$ 25,578,771
Coca-Cola Co.	472,587	$ 27,882,633

Table 8.22: Schedule of Investments for Diamonds Trust Series

Common Stocks	Shares	Value
Disney (Walt) Co.	472,587	$ 12,464,482
Du Pont (E.I.) de Nemours & Co.	472,587	$ 30,452,325
Eastman Kodak Co.	472,587	$ 32,578,966
Exxon Corp.	472,587	$ 35,000,975
General Electric Co.	472,587	$ 64,065,075
General Motors Corp.	472,587	$ 33,199,237
Hewlett Packard Co.	472,587	$ 35,000,975
Home Depot, Inc.	472,587	$ 35,680,318
Intel Corp.	472,587	$ 36,567,184
International Business Machines	472,587	$ 46,490,746
International Paper Co.	472,587	$ 24,869,891
Johnson & Johnson	472,587	$ 49,503,488
McDonald's Corp.	472,587	$ 19,494,214
Merck & Co., Inc.	472,587	$ 37,600,203
MicrosoftCorp.	472,587	$ 43,715,063
Minnesota Mining & Manufacturing Co.	472,587	$ 44,925,302
Morgan (J.P.) & Co., Inc.	472,587	$ 61,849,824
Philip Morris Cos., Inc.	472,587	$ 11,903,285
Procter & Gamble Co.	472,587	$ 49,562,562
SBC Communications, Inc.	472,587	$ 24,072,400
United Technologies Corp.	472,587	$ 28,591,513
Wal-Mart Stores, Inc.	472,587	$ 26,789,776
Total Investments--(Cost $1,049,298,154)		**$ 1,036,207,601**

The entire prospectus can be viewed at the Amex website for all the details on expenses and administrative details. For purposes of this book, it is sufficient to point out that the management fee is capped at 0.18% which is very reasonable.

What Are The Other Index Shares?

If you refer to **Appendix R: Various Index Shares**, you will notice by the names of the funds that almost any index in existence is represented. Certainly, all the major ones developed and tracked by Dow Jones, Standard and Poors, Frank Russell and Morgan Stanley are included. In the near future there will be even more to choose from.

When you look at this tremendous variety and diversity, ask yourself if you really need anything else to build a solid, diversified portfolio that allows you to sleep at night.

For Canadian Readers

Also of interest to our Canadian readers, the TSE300 index is well represented by TSE/S&P60 index participation units (i60's), which hold the top 60 stocks on the Toronto Stock Exchange. These units are similar to SPYDERS in concept, and are managed by Barclay's Global Investors for a very low management fee. They trade on Toronto under symbol XIU.

More information is available on BGI's website at www.bar-claysglobal.com.

Are there minimum dollar amounts required?

While there are really no minimums mandated on the purchase of index shares, you will pay a brokerage commission on each transaction. Because of this, we offer some guidelines on what makes sense for the average investor.

- If you have $10,000 or more for an individual transaction, it is more advantageous to use the DIA's or SPY's due to the lower management fee, which will partially offset any small commissions you must incur to buy them.
- If you have less than $10,000, you are better off with mutual funds because of the no-load status. This is because the commissions on a small amount of index shares could eat up a large portion of the gains made.

- On a total portfolio basis, with elements of domestic equity, foreign equity, and fixed income index shares combined with a cash component, we suggest a $20,000 to $25,000 minimum. This is because there are several commission charges incurred on the multiple purchases of index shares. Below this threshold, use mutual funds.

Index shares or index mutual funds are suitable and carry equal status when used inside a retirement account where there will be no tax implications. In a trading account where you are going to be paying the taxes on the distributions every year, the DIA's appear to be a better choice because you have more control over the realization of capital gains and only a portion of the dividends will be received through the part year you are holding them.

Index Investing Resources

For more information on indexing and index products in general, refer to these websites:

- www.indexfunds.com
- www.vanguard.com
- www.barclaysglobal.com
- www.waterhouse.com
- www.tdwaterhouse.ca
- www.tdbank.ca
- www.cibc.com
- www.ishares.com
- www.etrade.com
- www.schwab.com
- www.amex.com

Build Your Portfolio

The Annual Cycle and the Hot Cycles of the *Time In Time Out* system work independently. You can just choose one strategy that best suits your needs or use a combination of long-term and short-term strategies for a complete portfolio. You may even decide to include one or both of the strategies in your diversified portfolio of individual stocks. It comes down to how much involvement you want with your investments and what type of returns you want to achieve.

How exactly would you set up the new plan?

Assume for a moment that everything outlined in this book so far compels you to make a clean break from the way you invest today. You want to follow the Annual Cycle strategy and you wish to commit to an index portfolio exclusively.

The first thing you must do is identify what type of investor you are so that you can determine what portion of the portfolio to have in equity. Since this is not a financial planning book, it is assumed that you have been through this exercise already and have this concept firmly established. For reference, our personal benchmarks are:

1. An aggressive portfolio is 75% equity, 25% fixed income.
2. A balanced portfolio is 50% equity, 50% fixed income.

3. A conservative portfolio is 25% equity, 75% fixed income.

Since the *Time In Time Out* strategy replaces the equity portion of your portfolio, the decisions are kept to a minimum. Once you decide on the size of your equity portion, use the following sample portfolio.

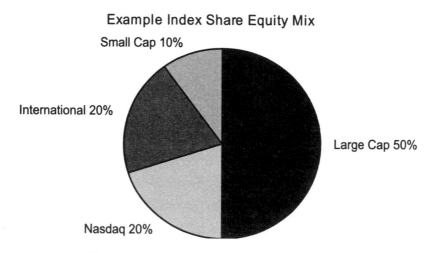

Example Index Share Equity Mix

Small Cap 10%

International 20%

Large Cap 50%

Nasdaq 20%

Figure 9.44: Example Index Share Equity Mix

Large Cap Equity 50%...use DIA's or SPY's
Small Cap Equity 10%...use Russell 2000 ishares IWM
Nasdaq Equity 20%...use Nasdaq tracking stock QQQ
International Equity 20%...use ishares MSCI (choose the countries you want)

You now own a broadly diversified global equity portfolio. Use this sample equity mix to enter the market on October 28th and then to sell it on either May 5th or July 19th. During the Time Out cycle, shift your money to *money-market fund* to earn interest while you wait for the next Time In date of October 28th.

The suggested equity mix shown is purely an example based on what may be appropriate for the average investor. You should consult your personal advisor for a detailed recommendation.

If you are not able to use index shares as the sample portfolio suggests, you may substitute index mutual funds in the same categories.

Recapping the Annual Cycle

Regardless of the investment vehicle you decide to use, Table 9.23 summarizes the actions that you should take and the specific dates that you should follow:

Table 9.23: Reviewing the Annual Cycle Action Dates

FOR CONSERVATIVE INVESTORS:		
Buy equity portfolio	*Sell equity portfolio*	*Hold money-market fund OR cash*
October 28	May 5	May 6 to October 27

FOR AGGRESSIVE INVESTORS:		
Buy equity portfolio	*Sell equity portfolio*	*Hold money-market fund OR cash*
October 28	July 19	July 20 to October 27

Part 3

Hot Cycles

This part of the book is for short-term investors who are looking for opportunities that have a greater probability of making money than the market average:

- **Hot Cycles—An Introduction:** introduces Hot Cycles.
- **Why You Should Use Hot Cycles:** outlines the benefits of using Hot Cycles.
- **Super Seven—The Hottest Days of the Month:** the seven best days that occur at the end of the month.
- **Fantastic Five:** five days in the mid-month that produce that produce above average returns.
- **Witches' Hangover:** the best day of the month to short the market.
- **Trading Around the Holidays:** outlines the best way to trade the profitable days before and after holidays.
- **Extended-Short Cycles:** the 100-Day Cycle and the 55-Day Cycle. These cycles are ideal for an investor looking for an opportunity that is longer than the Hot Cycles and shorter than the Annual Cycle.
- **Cool Tools and Implementation Strategies:** outlines options as an investment tool and develops a basic implementation strategy to combine the Annual Cycle with the Hot Cycles.

Hot Cycles—An Introduction

There are many books available on how to make money by short-term stock trading; this book is radically different. Most other short-term strategies require an investor to use graphs and complicated calculations. With Hot Cycles, all you need is a calendar. To beat the market, simply buy and sell on the predetermined dates identified throughout this part of the book. By knowing the best times of each month and year to invest, you can easily increase your profits. In addition, Hot Cycles offers intangible benefits that other systems cannot: decreased stress and a vacation away from the markets when they are typically headed into negative territory.

As stock brokers, we saw the market move in regular patterns and became very excited when we discovered the potential for increased profits. After extensive research, we concluded that the market was not random, as we had previously been taught. There were certain times of each month and year from 1950 to 1999, that consistently produced above average profits.

After analyzing all of the data, we developed Hot Cycles; practical short-term investment strategies that can be used by any investor. Because they are so easy to use, novice traders can start using Hot Cycles right away. Although our strategies are straightforward, they are extremely effective at producing above average returns and are an excellent tool for the professional trader. They can use our system exclusively, which we recommend, or use it in conjunction with their current methods.

Hot Cycles, being extremely flexible, can be used with almost any equity product and with any investment method. As most equities have similar trends to the market, you can continue using your current investment products. Also, the strategies identify the best time to be in the market, which can be used by investors for short-term trading, options investments, and longer-term investments.

To illustrate how you can benefit from Hot Cycles, we have focused on the Dow index. All of the graphs in Part Three are based upon this index unless otherwise noted. The same general trends that exist for the Dow, also apply to the S&P500, Nasdaq and the TSE300.

In this part of the book we will show you how to make money using the following Hot Cycle strategies:

- **Super Seven**—the last four days at the end of the month and the first three of the next month, that dominate the overall returns of the market.
- **Fantastic Five**—the five days in the mid-month area that provide above average returns.
- **Witches' Hangover**—the day after witching day (the day option contracts expire), the only time to short the market.
- **Extended-short cycles (55-Day and 100-Day Cycles)**—these periods, starting in late fall and ending early in the following year, produce above average returns.

To make your reading easier, we have included graphic symbols to highlight the key concepts:

Explains how to read a new graph.

Situations where an adjustment in the strategy is recommended.

Days to buy and sell.

Times where a strategy may not achieve optimal results and the investor is advised to take a break.

Statistical information for reference purposes.

Although you may not be familiar with the t-statistic, you might be familiar with the concept of what it measures. Very often, opinion polls are taken using surveys to determine what the public feels about a certain issue. The results are then published with a certain level of probability.

The t-statistic is used to illustrate the statistical significance of how much better our Hot Cycle days are compared to the market average. All of our short-term trading strategies have daily averages that are statistically significant from the market average.

When using Part Three, it is important that you consider your own personal objectives and experience, to decide on the appropriate strategies. Not all short-term investment strategies are equal. For example, the Super Seven has a stronger trend than the Fantastic Five on a monthly basis. If you are looking for just one short-term monthly cycle to trade, Super Seven would be the one to use. An example of a strategy for the very aggressive investor would be the Witches' Hang-over. This is the trading day after the expiry date of the option con-tracts. It has consistently produced negative returns and provides a great opportunity for aggressive traders to short the market. On the other hand, you may be looking to start a mid-term investment, in which case the 55-Day or the 100-Day Cycles would be ideal.

A trading strategy that is published in the newspapers every so often, is trading around the holidays. Although there has been some valid and interesting research done in this area, focusing on just trading around the holidays can be misleading. Typically, the returns are a result of the holidays occurring during the Super Seven days. Where appropriate, we have adjusted our Super Seven days to account for any legitimate holiday effects.

Choosing the best day of the week to invest is also another topic of public debate. Although the trends are interesting, we do not recommend that investors use them as part of their trading strategies because:

- Hot Cycle strategies are a lot more profitable
- Most investors are not interested in trading just one day
- Trading just on the "best days" of the week can put you into the market during the wrong times of the year.

For your interest we have included graphs of the average day of the week gains by decade, from 1953 to 1999, in **Appendix H: Weekday Gains by Decade**.

Why You Should Use Hot Cycles

Although a long-term investor can benefit from knowing when the Hot Cycles occur, it is the short-term investors that get the most use out of this information. Hot Cycles offer short-term investors benefits that others systems cannot: greater profits, fewer false sell orders when using stop-losses (defined on page 143) and an "investor vacation" away from the markets. When you put all of these benefits together, Hot Cycles is an excellent system that every short-term investor should use.

Greater Profits

The major advantage for investors using Hot Cycles is that it can generate greater profits compared with trying to short-term trade on an ad hoc basis.

The full magnitude of how well the Hot Cycle days have performed can only be realized by comparing them with the market daily average. In all cases, our short-term strategies have significantly and statistically outperformed this benchmark.

> **Market Daily Average**—The market daily average is the average gain of all market days. It includes every single day over the time period being analyzed. Even when the market daily average is being compared with a Hot Cycle strategy, every single day's performance of the market, including the Hot Cycle days' perfor-

mance, is included in the market daily average. We use
this benchmark throughout Part Three, unless otherwise stated, because it is the fairest and most conservative method for comparison purposes.

Other than our extended short-term cycles, our Hot Cycles
are in the market for only a few days each month. With the absolute
return not being a huge number, the benefits of our strategies may not
be initially clear. For example, if one of our strategies returns less
than 1% on a short-term trade, it may not seem worthwhile. However,
when you compare the return of our strategy with the market average
for a similar time period, the benefits become apparent. Our short-
term strategies typically return a multiple of the market average. For
example, the total return of the Super Seven strategy, is **285%** of the
markets' average seven day return from 1950 to 1999.

From the standpoint of the average investor, there are three
ways to profit from our strategies:

- If you are looking for a short-term investment that
  could be used every month, then the best way to do this
  is with one of our Hot Cycle strategies.
- If you believe that a stock or index is going to rally and
  are looking for an entry point, the best time for your
  investment is during our short cycles.
- If you want to really take advantage of the strategies
  and the potential to make a lot of money, options are an
  excellent tool. As options are only for very aggressive
  investors, it is advised that you perform a thorough
  investigation on how they work (see Chapter 17 for a
  basic description on their use). Using options lets you

generate very large profits within the date range of our short-cycles.

Less false sell orders, when using stop-losses

One of the important aspects of short-term trading is protecting your capital. Short-term traders will very often use a stop-loss order to accomplish this objective. A stop-loss order automatically sells your investment if it drops below a certain price. If you purchase a stock at $100, and place a stop-loss order at $95, your stock will automatically be sold if the price declines to $95. The rationale for a stop-loss order is that if the price is dropping, then you were wrong in your analysis to buy the stock. In this case, you are better off to suffer a small loss, rather than watch the price decline further, or wait to see if the stock will turn around.

The problem with using this strategy is that you can get whip-sawed (the unwanted action of selling on a stop-loss order, only to have the stock rebound back in price). This is not to say that using stop-loss orders is a bad strategy, but you can be taken out of the market when in hind sight you wish you were not.

Short-term investors using stop-loss orders appreciate their stocks going up in price right after they have made a buy, because it minimizes their exposure to being whipsawed. Hot Cycles can provide the initial boost in price that helps to reduce the chance of being whipsawed. Although the trader may not take advantage of the initial profit generated, it gives them a safety buffer. The price of the stock must now fall further for the initial stop-loss to be activated.

Hot Cycles Give You An Investor Vacation

If you want to be able to use short-term investment strategies for many years or even decades, it is important that you are able to take a vacation from your investments. If your whole life is centered around the markets, it is just a matter of time before you burn out. As stock brokers, we saw this happen time and time again to other brokers and very active trading clients. Using our system will help stop burn out and help you become a veteran investor.

Many investment systems in use today never give their subscribers a break. Investors are always waiting for the next signal to buy or sell. When they are in the market, they are anticipating a sell signal that could come at any time. When they are out of the market, they are anticipating a buy signal that could come at any time.

With Hot Cycles, you never have to wonder if you are going to have to buy or sell tomorrow. With all of the buy and sell dates predetermined, you know exactly when you should be in the market and when you should be out. Although the market will not always act as expected, there is no sense in participating during the times when the market is typically negative. Being out of the market at these times gives you that much-needed vacation and allows you to have a balanced life.

Super Seven—The Hottest Days of the Month

As stock brokers, we noticed that the market tended to go up at the end of each month. It did not happen every time, but it was frequent enough to attract our attention. When we set out to look for monthly trends that the average investor could use, the end of the month was the first place that we examined. What we found was incredible. *The last four days of each month and the first three days of the next month, which we have named the Super Seven days, produced huge returns compared with the average seven days in the market.* They were not just slightly better; they were a lot better. There were other short-term trends in the market, but there were none that repeated themselves so often and provided such a great opportunity. **If you want to use just one short-term trend, it would have to be the Super Seven.**

Discovering the potential of the Super Seven strategy starts by looking at a graph of the typical month for the Dow index from 1950 to 1999. Figure 12.45 is representative of the average trend over the last fifty years.

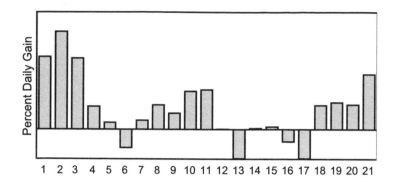

Figure 12.45: Dow Typical Month Trading Days,1950-1999

Typical Month 1950 to 1999

- *Average data for 600 months (1950 to 1999)*
- *Each column measures the average daily price gains or losses for a typical month for all 600 months*
- *Column #1 is the average daily gain for all of the first trading days of each month*
- *Column #2 is the average daily gain for all of the second trading days of each month and so on*
- *Since months have been adjusted for the typical month of 21 trading days, it can only be used to establish any trends.*

What is most astounding about this graph is that it is not flat. If the market were truly random over the long-term, you would expect to see all of the daily average gain columns the same height. This is definitely not the case. If the market has been going up over the last fifty years, how can there be certain days of the month which are negative? Easy, the market is not random: it has good days and bad days.

Placing two average months side-by-side in Figure 12.46, we can see that the days at the beginning of the month are individually as strong as the days at the end of the month. Together, they represent an incredible opportunity.

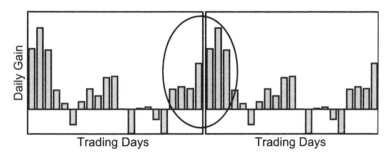

Figure 12.46:Two Typical Months Side-by-Side 1950-1999

The best way to accurately assess the strength of the Super Seven strategy is to compare the results of its trading days, with all of the days at the end of the month and the beginning of the next month. As a group, these days are referred to as the **end of the month days**, or **EOM days**. We use these trading days rather than calendar days because we can measure across every month on an equal basis.

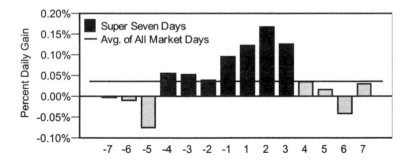

Figure 12.47: End of Month Trading Days 1950-1999

End of Month Days 1950-1999

- *Average month end for all 600 months from 1950 to 1999.*
- *Negative numbers on X-axis count down to the last trading days of the month*
- *Day -1 is the last trading day of the month*
- *Positive numbers on the X-axis count up from the first trading day of the next month*
- *Day 1 is the first trading day of the next month*
- *Super Seven days are the last four days of the month and the first three of the next month; shaded black*
- *Each column represents the average daily gain during the period specified*
- *The line, Average of All Market Days, illustrates the average daily gain for all days over the fifty year period.*

Figure 12.47 illustrates that the Super Seven days have much higher gains than the average daily gain of market over the fifty year period analyzed. What makes this strategy so unique is that all of the seven consecutive days in the Super Seven perform above the market average. There is no other group of seven days in the month that achieves this level of performance and provides such a huge opportunity for a profitable trade. Although there will be times when these days will produce a negative return, they have a higher likelihood of producing an above average return.

Figure 12.47 illustrates how much of an opportunity exists with the Super Seven. Using this graph, we will temporarily divide the Super Seven into two parts: the first three days and the last four.

- All of the first three days have slightly above average returns. These days alone are very good and present an opportunity in themselves. If you were looking for a three day strategy based on these days, you would expect above average returns.

- The last four days have significantly above average returns. These days also present an opportunity by themselves.
- When you put the two groups together, you end up with an excellent seven day opportunity.

By using the full seven days you benefit not only from above average returns on a daily basis, but also the compounding effect that would take place from one day to the next. Although this effect may seem small over seven days, if you were using a leveraged or option based investment strategy (discussed in Chapter 17), it could make a large difference.

To act on the Super Seven strategy, you would buy into the market fifteen minutes before the close of the fifth trading day before the end of the month. You would then hold for a full seven days, and sell fifteen minutes before the close on the third trading day of the next month.

We chose the Super Seven days based not only on the information in Figure 12.47, but also on a variety of other factors. To see the Super Seven results across decades, please refer to **Appendix I: Super Seven Daily Gain by Decade 1950-1999**.

Why does Super Seven Work?

It is fascinating to examine why Super Seven works. As trying to determine the causes is more art than science, there has been a lot of conjecture around the reasons. The main factor for the rise in stock prices is the increased money flow into the market that occurs at month end. There are several reasons why this happens:

- Window dressing for the clients
- Greater liquidity at pay time

- Brokers are busier at month end
- Automatic mutual fund purchase plans
- Employee savings plans and pension plans.

Window dressing for the clients

To see how window dressing works, it is important to take you into the world of the portfolio manager. Although portfolio managers are bound by rules and regulations about what types of investments they can purchase, they typically do not have to ask for permission on individual investments. They make their decisions based on their own criteria, as long as they stay within the mandate of the account that they are operating.

Window dressing is performed by portfolio managers to look good for the monthly or quarterly report. Just before the reporting deadline, they purchase stocks that are familiar to the investing public with their available cash. When clients receive their statements, they are more likely to think that their portfolio manager is doing well if they hold the "popular stocks" that everyone likes.

In the end, window dressing does little to change the value of the portfolio as it is done at the end of the reporting time. What does happen, however, is that new money is added into the market, driving up the price of stocks.

Greater Liquidity at Pay Time

As we have previously stated, money flowing into the market tends to increase the price of stocks. Where does all of this money come from? With investors getting paid on a monthly or bi-weekly basis, they tend to purchase stocks at these times. Some people may not believe that when you get paid can have an influence on the market, reasoning that wealthy people do not have to rely on their pay for investments. Although they may have more flexibility than the average person, wealthy people still tend to invest with their pay.

Brokers tend to be busier at month end

The brokerage industry will help place any money that has been slated for investments, but has not been placed by month end. Brokers regularly go through their clients' accounts at month end, checking for any "loose" cash to be invested. This money tends to be put into the market in the last few days of the month and the first few days of the next month, generating a higher money flow during this time.

Money is automatically invested into the market at month end

Another trend that has become popular is the automatic investment plan. With improved technology, banks and investment firms have been able to offer direct investing right from your pay. It is very convenient for the investor and a relatively painless way to save and invest. Once they have made the arrangements to purchase certain funds, they do not have to worry about what and when to buy. Also, they do not have to okay the transaction, as it happens automatically every month or with every pay.

Employee Savings Plans & Pension Plans

Most mid to large size companies now offer some type of Pension Plan, Group Retirement Plan or non-registered employee savings plan. Every year, more and more employees take advantage of these plans to save and invest money on a periodic basis.

Regardless of their exact nature, these plans all arrange for money to be deducted from the payroll and invested on a regular basis, usually twice a month. Since a large portion of the funds are designated for equity investments, the stock market receives a bi-weekly boost.

How much better are the Super Seven days

There are many different methods of measuring how much better the Super Seven days are relative to the market. In this part of the chapter we use three major measurements: daily average, seven day total return and percentage of Dow total growth. See "Different ways to measure the Super Seven strategy" on page 156, for an appendix list of other measurements.

Is the superiority of the Super Seven days Fluke or Fact?

Some skeptics may say that the results of the Super Seven strategy are a random fluke of the market. We have gone to great lengths analyzing data to test how significantly better the Super Seven days are compared to the market average. The Super Seven days are not a random fluke. They are both significantly and statistically better than the average market day.

 *From 1950 to 1999, the Super Seven days are significantly better than the average market day at an extremely high level. For t-statistic information see **Appendix L: Super Seven Statistics.***

We were not the first to discover the superiority of the end of the month effect, as there have been other academics that have come to the same conclusion. Depending on how long ago the study was done and what time period was analyzed, proponents of this strategy have advocated that there were four to seven superior days. We selected our seven days because they produced the best results, over many years.

Daily average superiority

The arithmetic daily average of the Super Seven days is vastly superior to the market daily average. From 1950 to 1999, the Super Seven days returned a daily average of 0.0938%, compared with 0.0355% for the market daily average. Figure 12.49 shows that on an average basis, a Super Seven day produces a return that is 264% of the market daily average, or is approximately two and half times better!

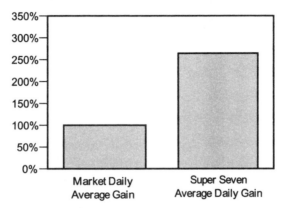

Figure 12.48: Daily Average Gain Comparison 1950-1999

This graph illustrates that on average, if you were to choose one Super Seven day and compare it with an average market day, you would do significantly better.

Compounded Dollar Growth captures most of the buy and hold returns

The Super Seven strategy has done a good job of capturing the majority of all of the market gains from 1950 to 1999. Using the Super Seven strategy, had you invested $1,000 at the end of the first month in 1950, made your gain, held cash until the next Super Seven days, invested, made your gain, and continued to do this until the end of 1999, you would have ended up with a total of $45,515. This would have accounted for 79% of the total market gain over the entire fifty years (see **Appendix K: Super Seven versus Buy and Hold Dow Jones Yearly Results** for yearly performance figures). Given that the Super Seven days account for about one-third of the total year, these results are remarkable.

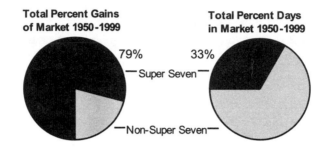

Figure 12.49: Total Market Gains and Participation Percentage

Figure 12.49 illustrates how much of the total market gain was accounted for by the Super Seven strategy and the percentage of the total market days.

Total Super Seven day return versus Total Average Market Seven day return

Another way to look at the Super Seven days is to compare the average return of the full seven days with an average seven day return of the market. These returns will be a little bit different than if you multiplied the daily averages of both groups by seven. The reason is simply the compounding effect that takes place over the seven days.

When a comparison is done on a full seven day return, the Super Seven days stand out even more than when the daily average comparison is used. The Super Seven days achieve a return rate of 0.6630% compared with the markets 0.2326%. This is a full 285% of the market return.

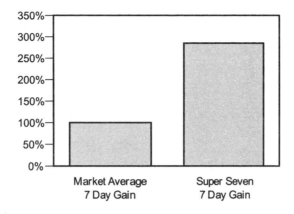

Figure 12.50: Total 7 Day Gain Comparison 1950-1999

The Super Seven days' overall return does not always beat the market average and it is not always positive. From 1950 to 1999, it was positive 64% of the time and beat the average seven day return 58% of the time. These numbers are not incredibly large, but they do contain a message. Although the number of times that the Super Seven beats the market is not spectacular, the gains are spectacular.

From 1950 to 1999, the Super Seven days overall return is significantly better than the average market seven day return, with a t-statistic of 4.43, it is significantly better.

How to use the Super Seven

Even after you realize how much better the Super Seven days are relative to the average market day, you may be wondering how you would use the strategy in a practical way. Many investors, unless they are investing a lot of money in the index, may not see the benefit of making 0.66% over seven days.

Everyone can benefit from the Super Seven strategy. You just have to use it in the way that it makes the most sense to you. There are four basic methods:

- Make a large investment in the index with the expectation of a gain at the end of the seven days.
- Use options as a leveraged investment. Despite the risk, there can be very large returns over a few days.
- Use the start date of the Super Seven as the start of a longer term investment.
- Purchase a stock that you believe has a chance of rallying strongly at the beginning of the Super Seven days. Individual stocks move up and down much more than the index. If the stock that you invest in is one of the top gainers over the seven days, your return will be greater than the index.

Although we have presented the four ways to use our strategy as being separate, you may wish to use any combination of these strategies depending on your investment style.

Different ways to measure the Super Seven strategy

There are many different ways to examine the effectiveness of the Super Seven days. For your reference we have included in the appendices:

- Decade graphs—**Appendix I: Super Seven Daily Gain by Decade 1950-1999**
- Monthly graphs—**Appendix J: Super Seven Daily Gain by Month 1950-1999**
- t-statistics, gain and frequency table—**Appendix L: Super Seven statistics**

- Yearly compound average data—**Appendix K: Super Seven versus Buy and Hold Dow Jones Yearly Results**

Profitable Adjustments

There are three simple adjustments that we recommend for greater profits. For further implementation details, other than what are listed below, see **Implementation Strategies** at the end of this chapter. For return analysis regarding the holidays, see chapter 15 **Trading Around the Holidays**. For simplicity, all of the return and frequency calculations in Part Three of this book do **not** make these three adjustments:

- **Thanksgiving** adjustment in November—the day before and the day after Thanksgiving have had daily average gains nine times better than the market average.

   When the day before Thanksgiving occurs within the Super Seven days, use the regular Super Seven strategy. Be in the market for the last four trading days of the month and the first three trading days of the next month.

   When the day before Thanksgiving occurs **before** the Super Seven days, be in the market a full day before Thanksgiving. In this case, you would be in the market for more than seven trading days, as the sell date still remains three trading days into the next month.

- **Christmas** adjustment in December—the day before Christmas has had daily average gains nine times better than the market average, and the day after Christmas has had gains seven times greater than the market average.

Be in the market for the full day before Christmas. You will be in the market for more than seven days, as the sell date still remains three trading days into the next month.

- **Annual Off-cycle** adjustment—take a break from using the strategy during the Annual off-cycle months of July, August and September.
- For more details on how to implement these three changes, see the information at end of the chapter.

Are the Best Days at the Month End Moving?

There has been some speculation as to whether the end of the month effect, which the Super Seven days capitalize on, has been starting earlier over the last several decades. The theory behind this is that more and more professional traders are taking advantage of the end of the month strategy by buying earlier, causing the best seven day period to start earlier. Figure 12.51 analyzes when the best seven day period around the end of the month has occurred, from 1930 to 1999.

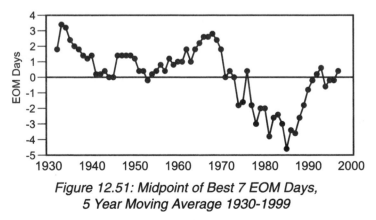

Figure 12.51: Midpoint of Best 7 EOM Days,
5 Year Moving Average 1930-1999

The Y-axis measures the best possible seven day midpoint. For example, if in any given year the value is -1, then out of all of the possible consecutive seven day combinations around the end of the month the best seven days would be from four days before the month end to three days into the next month. If the value was +1, then the best possible seven days would be two days before the end of the month to five days into the next month. A five year moving average has been used to smooth the line so that any trends would be apparent.

Until the 1970's, the best seven day period was skewed to the beginning of the new month. The mid-point of the seven days shifted to the end of the month in the 1980's, and the best seven days started earlier. In the 1990's, the mid-point of the seven days moved back to its long-term average.

Although we know that the end of the month is stronger than the rest of the month, in any given month it is not possible to pick the best days. In some months, it may be five days or eight days, or any number of days that perform above the market average. Also, these days as a group may be more concentrated in the next month, rather than the end of the current month, or vice versa.

As the number of above average days fluctuate from month to month and year to year, Super Seven is the best strategy to capture the end of the month effect. It has been structured with the correct number of days to capture the gains that occur at the end of the month. Also, it is also centered on the last day of the month, which allows for any shift in the group of days moving slightly from month to month.

Implementation Strategies

Buy & Sell Days

- *Buy fifteen minutes before the end of the fifth last trading day of the month*
- *Sell fifteen minutes before the close of the market on the third trading day of the next month*

Example*   January

Sun	Mon	Tue	Wed	Thur	Fri	Sat
//	//	//	//	//	//	//
21	22	23	24	(25)	26	27
28	29	30	31			

1) Buy 15 min before market close on Jan. 25th

2) Hold for 7 days starting on Jan. 26th

	February		1	2	3	
4	(5)	6	7	8	9	10
13	14	15	16	17	18	19

3) Sell 15 min. before market close on Feb. 5th

4) Repeat at the end of Feb.

▭ Super Seven days

* If January 29th were a weekend day, you would purchase one day earlier to make sure that you were in for the full seven days. If February 5th were a weekend day, you would sell on the 6th.

Omission Recommendations

- *Omit the Annual off-cycle months of July, August and September.*
- *Super Seven should be used during the same months that the Annual Cycle Time In period is used.*

The Santa Claus Adjustment

- *Buy fifteen minutes before market close on the second day before Christmas.*
- *No adjustment is needed for the sell date, as it still remains three trading days into the next month.*

Thanksgiving Adjustment

- *If the day before Thanksgiving occurs before the Super Seven date range, buy 15 minutes before market close on the Tuesday before the Thanksgiving holiday.*
- *If the day before Thanksgiving occurs during the Super Seven days, use the regular Super Seven strategy.*
- *No adjustment is needed for the sell date in either case, as it still remains three trading days into the next month.*

Table 12.24: Months To Use The Super Seven Strategy

Month	Use Super Seven
January	Yes
February	Yes
March	Yes
April	Yes
May	Yes
June	Yes
July	No
August	No
September	No
October	Yes
November	Yes—see special case of Thanksgiving adjustment
December	Yes—see special case of Santa Claus adjustment

In summary, we see that the Super Seven days:

- Provide above average returns
- Are more frequently positive than the average seven day periods
- Achieved 79% of total market return from 1950 to 1999
- Recommended months are October to June inclusive
- Include Thanksgiving and Christmas holiday adjustments.

Fantastic Five

If you are an aggressive investor, you do not have to limit yourself to using the Super Seven days. You can take advantage of another group of positive days that start on the second Friday of each month and last for a total of five trading days. This cluster of days produces positive returns that on a daily average basis, are beaten only by the Super Seven days. Although this strategy is not rated as highly as the Super Seven, there is still a lot of money to be made.

If we examine the typical month, we can see that the market tends to rise around the middle of the month (see Figure 13.52). This graph is based upon 21 trading days. Some months have more trading days and others have less; therefore, it can only be used as an approximation to see the general trend. Prior to 1953, the market was open on Saturdays. Since the Fantastic Five strategy is day of the week related, only data after and including 1953 was considered.

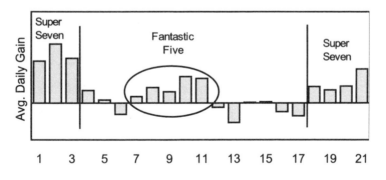

Figure 13.52: Typical Month Trading Days 1953-1999

Although this graph is used for approximation purposes only, you can see that other than the days in the Super Seven and the Fantastic Five regions, the rest of the month appears to be negative.

How we found the Fantastic Five

To find the best way to capitalize on the mid-month effect, we developed many different scenarios using calendar and trading days. With the Super Seven strategy, we used trading days because the number of trading days left in the month was causing the market to move. When we tried the same approach to capture the mid-month effect; the results were mildly positive. After speculating that the causes of money flowing into the markets during mid-month might be calendar day based, we decided to analyze the mid-month effect from this angle. This ended up being the right way, as the results were much stronger. The best strategy to capture the mid-month effect is to use the **Fantastic Five: the five trading days starting on the second Friday of the month.**

How good are the Fantastic Five days?

If an investor were looking for two different strategies to use in a month and they had already invested in the Super Seven days, the next best choice would be the Fantastic Five. Figure 13.53 shows that from 1953 to 1999, the Fantastic Five days have performed very well relative to all of the days in the month and extremely well relative to all of the market days excluding the Super Seven. The Fantastic Five had a daily average return of 0.0636%, the market daily average 0.0350% and the market daily average with the Super Seven days excluded was 0.0072%.

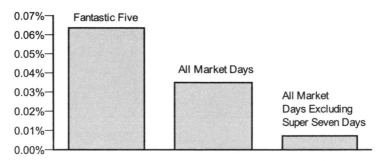

Figure 13.53: Average Daily Gain Comparison 1953-1999

 Fantastic Five 1953-1999

* *Average of all market days—average daily gain for all days of the year from 1953 to 1999.*

* *Average of all market days excluding Super Seven days— average daily gain for all days of the year excluding the Super Seven Days, from 1953 to 1999.*

If we look at Figure 13.54 on a daily basis, we can see that all five days of the Fantastic Five have had average or above average performance (day three is average and the rest are above). What is interesting to note is the difference between the Fantastic Five days and the average of all market days excluding the Super Seven. The difference is huge.

The magnitude of how well the Fantastic Five strategy has performed is apparent when we remove the positive performance of the Super Seven strategy from the market daily average. The average, represented by the solid line in Figure 13.54 drops to a much lower level, represented by the dotted line. All of the Fantastic Five returns are far superior to the remaining average. On this basis, the only two times that you should be performing short-term trades are during either the Super Seven or the Fantastic Five cycles.

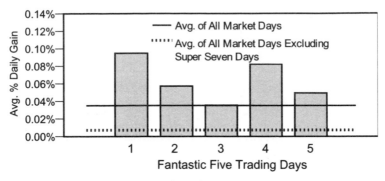

Figure 13.54: Fantastic Five Daily Averages 1953-1999

Fantastic Five Days—Day #1 is the second Friday of the month, Day #2 the next trading day and so on. When the days are shown separately, each column measures the average daily gain for that day, across all months for every year from 1953 to 1999.

The Fantastic Five has not always been extremely positive. It has only been in the last several decades that these days have created the mid-month effect. We have examined data from 1953 to be consistent with our previous analysis.

 From 1953 to 1999, the Fantastic Five days are significantly better than the average market day. For more t-statistic information see **Appendix M: Fantastic Five Statistics**

The Fantastic Five By Decade

The following three graphs show the success of the Fantastic Five strategy by decade, for the 1970's, 1980's and 1990's.

Figure 13.55 shows that in the 1990's, the average Fantastic Five day produced returns that were more than double the average day, with or without the Super Seven days factored in.

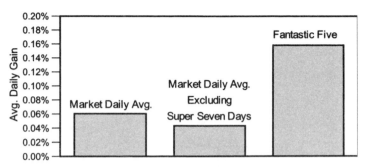

Figure 13.55: Fantastic Five Comparison 1990's

<u>Actual Results</u>

Fantastic Five daily average = 0.1583 %
Market daily average = 0.0604 %
Market daily average excluding Super Seven Days =
0.0432 %

In the 1980's, the average Fantastic Five day return fell just short of the market daily average due to the incredible performance of the Super Seven days. When the effect of the Super Seven was removed, the Fantastic Five produced returns of more than 500% greater than the remaining days.

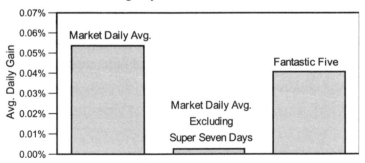

Figure 13.56: Fantastic Five Comparison 1980's

<u>Actual Results</u>

Fantastic Five daily average = 0.0407 %
Market daily average = 0.0536 %
Market daily average excluding Super Seven Days =
0.00254 %

The final graph, Figure 13.57, shows that in the 1970's, the average Fantastic Five day return fell just short of the market daily average. It is interesting to note that when the Super Seven days' gains are removed, the average return of the remaining days is actually *negative*.

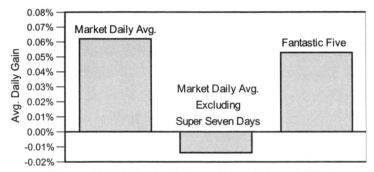

Figure 13.57: Fantastic Five Comparison 1970's

<u>*Actual Results*</u>

Fantastic Five daily average = 0.0528 %
Market daily average = 0.062 %
Market daily average excluding Super Seven Days = - 0.0139 %

There are different ways to examine the effectiveness of the Fantastic Five. For your reference we have included in the appendix:

- Decade graphs- **Appendix N: Fantastic Five Daily Gain by Decade 1950-1999**
- Monthly graphs- **Appendix O: Fantastic Five Daily Gain by Month 1950-1999**
- t-statistic, daily gain and frequency table- **Appendix M: Fantastic Five Statistics**

Implementation Strategies

- *Buy 15 minutes before the close of the market on the Thursday before the second Friday of the month*
- *Sell 15 minutes before the close of the market five trading days later*

Example			January			
Sun	Mon	Tue	Wed	Thur	Fri	Sat
		1	2	3	4	5
6	7	8	9	(10)	11	12
13	14	15	16	(17)	18	19

▭ Fantastic Five days

1) Buy 15 min before market close on Jan. 10th

2) Hold for 5 days starting on Jan. 11th

3) Sell 15 min. before market close on Jan. 17th

4) Repeat in Feb.

Special Case

When the Fantastic Five strategy starts early in the month, there is a chance that the it will come close to starting when the Super Seven strategy is ending. The investor should decide if they want to continue holding their Super Seven position over the short gap between the two strategies.

Omission Recommendations

Omit the Annual off-cycle months of August, September and October (July is acceptable to use, as the Fantastic Five typically finishes before the final exit date of the Annual Cycle).

Witches' Hangover

Up to this point in the book we have discussed buying when the market is down and selling when the market is up, only to reinvest again when the market is down. Witches' Hangover is a different method. It provides an opportunity for the very aggressive investor to short the market, or make money on the market's decline. We know that most investors do not want to short the market because of the greater risks involved, but for those that do, we want to equip them with the best possible strategy.

> **Shorting**—the process of selling stock before you have bought it, in the attempt of buying the stock at a lower price in the future and pocketing the difference between the buy and the sell price.

We have coined the term **"Witches' Hangover"** to describe **the trading day after witching day, which is typically negative**. This is the best time to short the market, as it suffers the after-effects of the preceding volatile witching day. Witching day is the third Friday of each month, or the trading day before if Friday is a holiday. On this day each month, stock and index options expire. In addition to these options, the futures options expire at the end of each quarter. When all three expire at the end of each quarter, this day is known as triple witching day. All witching days are typically volatile because investors are buying and selling to cover their positions on their

options. For the average investor this can be a day of concern, however, for the informed investor this can be a day of opportunity.

A brief history of options and witching days

First of all, the options we are discussing are not the options
that employees and executives receive for working at a company. The
options that we are focusing on are traded in the market like stocks
and have nothing to do with status of employment.

When you buy a call option, you are buying the right to purchase the underlying security at a certain price up to a certain date in
the future. The basic advantage of buying an option is to leverage
your money. It is possible to make very large amounts of money using
relatively small amounts of money up front. On the other hand, you
can lose everything that you invest. Before considering the use of
options we recommend that you read other books on their use and
seek professional advice. Although there is a greater degree of risk,
more investors are using options to take advantage of short-term
opportunities. They are an ideal investment vehicle for short-term
traders.

Witching day tends to be volatile because investors are selling and buying stocks to cover their option positions. Despite its volatility, witching day ends up only slightly negative. We are starting our
analysis in 1974 because this is the year that the Chicago Board of
Exchange (CBOE) created the first full scale options exchange. From
1974 to 1999 on witching day itself, the Dow has had only a small
loss of 0.015%.

On the other hand, Witches' Hangover, has ended with an
average daily loss of 0.15%. At first glance this number may not seem
like much, but relative to the average Dow day it presents an attractive trading opportunity.

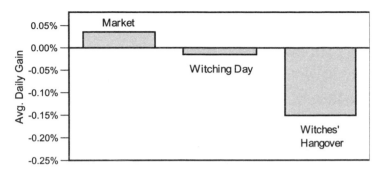

Figure 14.58: Witches' Hangover Daily Average Performance 1974-99

<u>*Actual Results*</u>
Witches' Hangover daily average = - 0.159 %
Market daily average = 0.0355 %
Witching day =   - 0.015 %

Figure 14.58 illustrates the magnitude of the decline that typically happens on Witches' Hangover, relative to the performance of witching day and the market daily average.

Figure 14.59 illustrates the performance of Witches' Hangover, relative to the surrounding days.

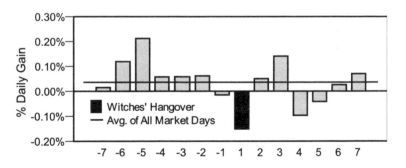

Figure 14.59: Days Before and After Witches' Hangover 1974-1999

If you look at the typical month shown in Figure 14.60, Witches' Hangover falls one half to two thirds the way through, which is the most negative part of the month. Caution is advised in using this strategy when the third Friday is close to the end of the month. For example, if the first of the month starts on a Saturday, there are relatively few days after Witches' Hangover before the Super Seven has its positive effect.

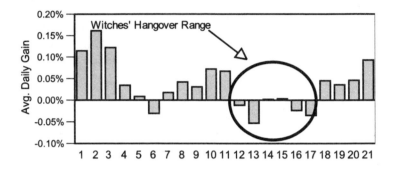

Figure 14.60: Typical Month Trading Days 1974-1999

From 1974 to 1999, the Witches' Hangover days, having a t-statistic of -2.13, are significantly negative compared to the average market day.

As Witches' Hangover typically falls on a Monday, it makes sense to compare its performance with the average Monday performance. Witches' Hangover had a loss of 0.151% versus the average Monday, which had a gain of 0.026%. For a more conservative comparison, we excluded the Mondays that occurred during the Super Seven, as these days would have given Mondays' performance a positive boost. Non-Super Seven Mondays had a return of 0.008%, which is still substantially more positive, relative to Witches' Hangover (see Figure 14.61).

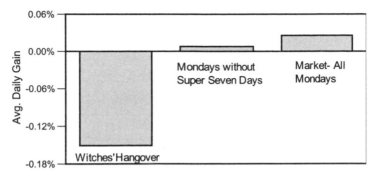

Figure 14.61: Monday Comparison 1974-1999

Witches' Hangover has worked well over the decades (See **Appendix P: Witches Hangover Daily Gain by Decade**). However, in the roaring bull market of the 1990's, it has not performed as well. In a strong bull market, there is less opportunity to short the market.

On a monthly basis Witches' Hangover is in negative territory for ten out of the twelve months, with only January and May producing small positive returns (see Figure 14.62). Although October has the largest negative loss, caution is advised as the market typically rallies very strongly at the end of the month. If you are looking to short the market with the possibility of extending your date out in the future, this would not be the month for this strategy.

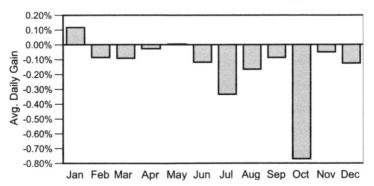

Figure 14.62: Witches' Hangover By Month 1974-1999

*Table 14.25: Witches' Hangover Average
Performance Across Months—1974-1999*

Month	Return	Month	Return	Month	Return
January	0.117%	May	0.0042%	September	-0.0873%
February	-0.0862%	June	-0.119%	October	-0.770%
March	-0.092%	July	-0.335%	November	-0.0501%
April	-0.0278%	August	-0.166%	December	-0.126%

Implementation Strategy

Buy and Sell Dates

- *Take a short position 15 min. before the close of the market on Witching day*

- *Cover your position 15 min. before the close of the market on Witches' Hangover*

Example   August

Sun	Mon	Tue	Wed	Thur	Fri	Sat
		1	2	3	4	5
6	7	8	9	10	11	12
13	14	15	16	17	18	19
20	21	22	23	24	25	26

1) Take short position 15 minutes before market close on Aug 18th

2) Cover position 15 minutes before market close on Aug 21th

3) Repeat in Sep.

⬜ Witches' Hangover

Trading Around the Holidays

There is usually a lot of "noise" in the newspapers around holiday time as to whether the stock market has traditionally gone up or down, before and after the holidays. To a large degree, these newspapers are missing the point. It is difficult to tell how much of the positive trend for the holidays is due to the holiday itself, and how much is due to the end of the month effect. Although investing before and after the holidays presents a profitable opportunity, we concluded from our extensive analysis that the best strategy is to trade the Super Seven days with the exception of making an adjustment for Thanksgiving and Christmas.

When the holiday falls in the Super Seven range, it tends to have a stronger performance. When it falls outside of this range, its performance tends not to be as strong. If you examine Table 15.26, you will see that five out of the nine holidays can fall within the Super Seven range of days. The first holiday that does not fall within the Super Seven range is Martin Luther King Jr. Day. It is impossible to determine if this holiday has a trend as the market has only been closed for this day, starting in 1998. The second holiday, President's Day, does not demonstrate a strong noticeable trend. It is possible that this days' performance is negatively affected because it can occur on Witches' Hangover day. The third holiday is Easter, or Good Friday in particular. This holiday is different than the rest because it is based on the full pascal moon and the date (or even month) can move around, depending on the year. The fourth holiday, Christmas, has typically provided an excellent opportunity for greater profits, therefore, we have adjusted the Super Seven strategy to include this holiday.

Table 15.26: Holiday Overlap with the Super Seven Days

Holiday	Overlap with Super Seven
New Year's Day	Possible Super Seven Day
Martin Luther King Jr. Day	Market has only been closed for this holiday only since 1998
President's Day	No large trend with trading days around holiday
Good Friday	Moves around depending on the Full Pascal Moon, and can be the day after Witching day
Memorial Day	Possible Super Seven Day
Independence Day	Possible Super Seven Day
Labor Day	Possible Super Seven Day
Thanksgiving Day	Possible Super Seven Day- Super Seven strategy adjusted to include the day before Thanksgiving (when it falls outside of the Possible Super Seven days)
Christmas Day	Possible Super Seven Day-Super Seven strategy adjusted to include the day before and after Christmas

Historically, the days before and after the Christmas and Thanksgiving holidays have produced above average returns with strong frequency numbers (see graphs 15.63 and 15.64 respectively). It makes sense with these two holidays to extend the Super Seven strategy.

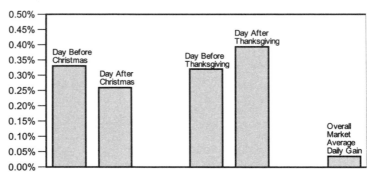

Figure 15.63: Average Holiday Gains 1950-1999

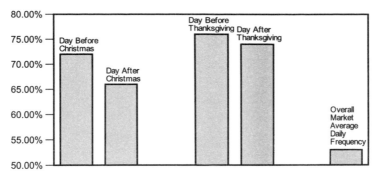

Figure 15.64: Average Holiday Frequencies 1950-1999

From Figures 15.63 and 15.64, you can see that these holidays produce powerful results. Both the frequency and the gains are far superior to market averages.

Table 15.27: Holiday Gains & Frequency 1950-1999

	Christmas		*Thanksgiving*		*Market Average*
	Before	**After**	**Before**	**After**	—
Gain	0.33%	0.26%	0.32%	0.39	0.036%
Frequency	72%	66%	76%	74%	53%

For implementation of the Super Seven strategy with these two holiday adjustments, please refer to page 160.

Extended-Short Cycles

This chapter is for the investor that is looking for calendar investment strategies that are shorter than the Annual Cycle and longer than the previously discussed Hot Cycles. The two cycles that meet these requirements are the 100-Day Cycle and the 55-Day Cycle. Both cycles will not always contain the same number of days as their names imply, because they are an average of their cycle length that changes from year to year. Both occur in late fall and early winter, which is the sweet spot of the market: the spot where the best returns are frequently made. They can be used in combination with any of the other cycles discussed in this book, but they are perfect for the investor who wants to find the right time to increase or leverage their equity exposure.

The traditional "buy, hold and close your eyes" strategy dictates that the best time to buy into the market is when you have the money. Despite this, many investors that have extra money sitting on the sidelines want to know the best time to put new money into the market to get maximum returns. Earlier in the book, we clearly outlined that the best time to be in the market is from October 28th to either May 5th or July 19th, depending on whether you are a conservative or aggressive investor. The 100-Day and 55-Day Cycles are both contained within this date range, but they allow an investor to exit the market earlier.

100-Day Cycle

- *Buy 15 min. before market close on October 27th*
- *Sell 15 min. before market close on the third trading day of February*

55-Day Cycle

- *Buy 15 min. before market close on the trading day before the second Friday of December*
- *Sell 15 min. before market close on the third trading day of February*

The best way to think about these cycles is in the context of the Annual Cycle. The Annual Cycle is the longest cycle and starts on October 28th. The 100-Day Cycle starts at the same time, but ends at the beginning of February. The 55-Day Cycle starts in mid December and lasts until the beginning of February.

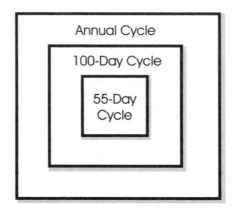

Figure 16.65, illustrates that the 100-Day Cycle captures most of the yearly advance of the market. The 55-Day Cycle has a steeper sloped line indicating that it captures the period of the strongest gains.

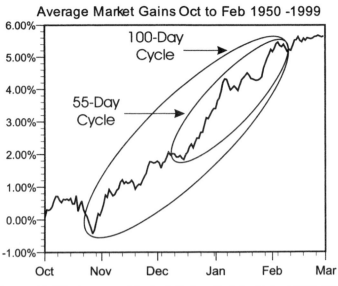

Figure 16.65: Average Market Gains Oct. to Feb. 1950-1999

For the 100-Day and 55-Day Cycles by decade, see **Appendix Q: 100-Day and 55-Day Cycles by Decade**.

If we look at the monthly positive frequencies in Table 16.28 (percentage of time that the month is positive), we can see that the 100-Day Cycle and the 55-Day Cycle incorporate months that have the highest probability of positive gains: November 68%, December 72% and January 70%.

Table 16.28: Monthly % Positive 1950-1999

Month	Freq. Positive	Month	Freq. Positive
January	70.00%	July	60.00%
February	58.00%	August	56.00%
March	64.00%	September	38.00%
April	64.00%	October	56.00%
May	52.00%	November	68.00%
June	52.00%	December	72.00%

Performance of the 100-Day and 55-Day Cycles

To be consistent with the previous measurements, average daily gains were used to evaluate the 100-Day and 55-Day Cycles. Figure 16.66 illustrates the average daily gain for the 100-Day, 55-Day and Annual Cycle (Time In portion—October 28th to July 19th), and compares them with the Dow on a buy and hold basis.

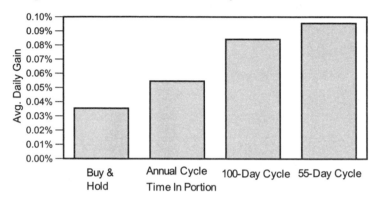

Figure 16.66: Average Daily Gains By Strategy 1950-1999

Table 16.29: Average Daily Gains by Strategy, 1950-1999

Market buy and hold	Annual Cycle Time In Portion	100-Day Cycle	55-Day Cycle
0.0355 %	0.0546 %	0.0842 %	0.0962 %

Table 16.29 illustrates that the average daily gain for the 100-Day, 55-Day Cycles and Annual Cycle, are vastly superior to the buy and hold result. As the cycles decrease in time exposure to the market, they increase in terms of average daily gain; indicating they are increasing in efficiency.

Another way to measure the results of the 100-Day and 55-day Cycles is in terms of what percentage of the total Dow gain they achieve in an average year. The following table shows the actual numbers.

Table 16.30: Extended Short Cycles Average Gains versus the Dow index for 1950 to 1999

	Actual Average Gain	Percentage of Dow Gain
100-Day Cycle	5.78%	59.5%
55-Day Cycle	3.28%	33.7%

The 100-Day Cycle is responsible for a very large portion of the total yearly gain for the Dow. The 55-Day Cycle result shows that it is responsible for one-third of the average yearly Dow gain. These results are excellent considering the very small amount of time the cycles are at work during the course of a year. Figure 16.67 shows the participation rate (amount of time invested in the Dow) for each of the cycles, compared with the Dow.

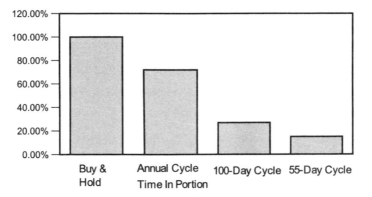

Figure 16.67: Percent Market Participation 1950-1999

Summing up the 100-Day and 55-Day Cycles, we see that:

- They are highly efficient in producing returns
- They capture the best period of the year
- They give you minimum time exposure to the market.

Cool Tools &
Implementation Strategies

Hot Cycles can be used in a number of different ways by a variety of different investors. They can be used with stocks, market indices, mutual funds, or options. You can use them in conjunction with your current investment method, or to modify equity exposure within your given risk tolerance.

Although we would like to think that everyone should concentrate primarily on using our techniques, we know that this will not always happen. Some dedicated investors will stick closely to our system and will benefit in the long run from above average returns. Others will continue to use their current methodology of investing and will use our system to complement their decisions.

For the investor that wants to continue picking their own stocks, Hot Cycles is a very valuable resource. If you are looking to execute a short-term trade at the right time with a stock that you think has good potential, why not wait until the Super Seven or the Fantastic Five cycles? Doing so will put the probability of making a sound decision on your side.

If you are invested during the Annual Cycle, how do you use one of the Hot Cycles? If you are a conservative investor, perhaps the idea of short-term trading does not appeal to you. In this case, you could still use the Hot Cycle guidelines to vary your exposure to equities. If you are an aggressive investor, however, you may want to pursue one of the Hot Cycle opportunities in a variety of ways. The balance of this chapter will detail the methods you can use to derive maximum gains from the Hot Cycles.

Use Hot Cycles To Tailor Your Equity Exposure

If you decide that you want to be invested for the Annual Cycle, but you also want to take advantage of the 100-Day or 55-Day Cycles, there is a strategy that you can use. It is the same one that many investment managers use: adjust your equity holdings to your expectations of the market. If you are to follow this strategy the first important step is to determine your maximum equity exposure based upon your risk tolerances. The next step would be to determine the average amount the equity exposure that meets your long-term comfort level.

Using Figure 17.68 as an example, if you would like to have 50% to 70% of your portfolio in the market, then the following strategy would make sense. Invest 70% in equities starting on October 28th. This would be the start date for both the Annual Cycle and the 100-Day Cycle. When the 100-Day Cycle finishes at the beginning of February, reduce you equity position to the average level of 50%. On your Annual Cycle exit date in July, you would then move to cash and earn interest on your money.

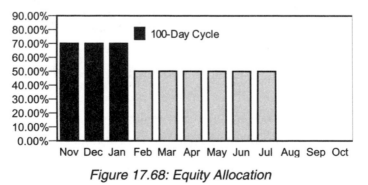

Figure 17.68: Equity Allocation

Use Hot Cycles For Stock Trading

If you are a trader purchasing a stock for the short-term during a strong rally, you want the stock to go up by more than the market. A larger percentage gain frequently occurs for individual stocks compared to the market as a whole. Using the Super Seven or the Fantastic Five cycles as a guideline can help you zero in on the most positive times to perform your trade.

We tested this effect using historical data for the market indices and two individual stocks mentioned earlier in the book; Hewlett Packard and 3M. The following graphs show a comparison of these two stocks with the Dow and S&P500 indices during the Fantastic Five Cycle in November, 1999.

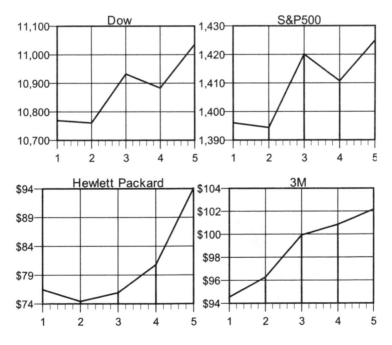

Figure 17.69: Individual Stocks versus Indices

Figure 17.69 illustrates the effect of strong percentage gains in individual stocks occurring during the Hot Cycles. Both Hewlett Packard and 3M outperformed the indices in the Fantastic Five days.

Dow	4.15 %
S&P500	3.11 %
3M	9.98 %
Hewlett Packard	27.77 %

This comparison illustrates the potential for large and rapid price appreciation with individual stocks. The top performers in any given short-term cycle will outpace the index by a wide margin. Not all stocks will experience these types of gains, and the magnitude of the gains will vary from month to month. Which stocks to choose is for you to decide; Hot Cycles can tell you when to do it.

Options—The Really Big Money

If you are looking for bigger profits, the use of options are the perfect tool. While there is the potential for huge gains, there is more risk in using options compared with stocks, as you could potentially lose all of the money that you invest. Since option trading is a higher risk strategy designed for aggressive investors, we advise to you seek professional guidance regarding their suitability to your objectives and risk tolerance. It is also important to seek guidance regarding the portion of your portfolio to use with an options strategy. Typically, only a very small portion of an aggressive trader's portfolio is dedicated to options trading.

The purpose of this section is to give you a very basic idea of how options work. When you purchase a call option, you are leveraging your money in the expectation that the market or your stock will go up. A put option is the reverse; you are expecting the market to go down.

With a call option, you are acquiring the right to buy a stock or index at a specified price on a specified date. If the underlying stock or index price goes up by several percentage points, it is possible to make a profit that will give you many times your original investment. This is leverage at work. On the other hand if the stock goes down below the specified price, your option contract expires worthless and you lose all of your investment. You do not have to wait the entire period until the option expiry date, as it is possible to trade these options during any day the market is open, at whatever price supply and demand dictates.

Call options are the type used most frequently with *Time In Time Out*, because the Annual Cycle Time In period, Super Seven, Fantastic Five, 100-Day and 55-Day Cycles all identify when the market is most likely to go up. Therefore, call options are the appropriate vehicle for capturing their superior gains.

Put options are only used in the Time Out portion of the Annual Cycle if desired, and with the Witches' Hangover strategy, as the market is most likely to decline during these periods.

Although option contracts can be purchased to expire up to two years in the future, they all expire on the third Friday of the month. The longer the time period is to the expiry date, generally the larger the premium that an investor expects to pay. If an option contract goes beyond one year, it is considered a LEAP.

If you already use options to invest, Hot Cycles can boost your profits. For example, if you are looking to invest for a few days it would make sense to buy a call option at the start of the Super Seven or Fantastic Five days, and sell it at the end of the cycle. If you have not used options yet, but are considering doing so in the future, Hot Cycles can act as a roadmap for your activities.

How and When To Use Options

Previously it was explained that the beginning of the Annual and 100-Day Cycles are very powerful times to be invested due to superior market advances. When the positive influences of the month of November and the Fantastic Five days are added, you have an incredibly strong period. We tracked the performance of the Dow 10,800's, December call options, during the Fantastic Five period in November to illustrate the gains that are possible.

At the beginning of the Fantastic Five, this call option could be purchased for $2.50, but when the Dow started advancing rapidly on the second and third day of the cycle, the option price rose to $3.75; a gain of 50%! By the time the five trading days had concluded, the option had risen to $4.375; a gain of 70%. This contrasts with the Dow gain of 4.1%, which would ordinarily be considered fantastic. *Because of the leverage, the return from the option outperformed the Dow index by 1700%. That's the power of leverage.*

Time In Time Out: Conclusion

As human beings, sometimes we are oblivious to our surroundings. We fail to see the patterns of nature or human behavior unfolding before our eyes. When this happens, all seems random.

For us, this was the case with the stock market. Until we spent one year of our lives researching its historical patterns, we believed that it was unpredictable. We now know better.

The *Time In Time Out* system was developed based on our discovery that profitable patterns have been re-occurring for a long time. Using our system will alter your perspective on the stock market: you will be able to see order instead of chaos.

Your decisions will based on probabilities, rather than on speculation, and investing will become systematic. While the patterns may not work all the time, they will work most of the time. As a result, you will enjoy better than average returns with lower risk.

We hope you prosper from using our system in the future and take advantage of the time when you are not invested to enjoy the other important things in life.

Appendix A: Conservative Time In Exit Date

The following table illustrates the findings for the May 5th exit date for conservative investors since 1953. The numbers are presented on a cumulative basis to show the long-term benefit of a repetitive plan, based on a $100,000 original investment.

Table Headings

Date = calendar day of portfolio transaction, in month/day/year format

Action = either buying or selling the market index

Dow = Dow index level

$ Dow = total dollars of market gain produced by investing with buy and hold in the Dow index

$TT = total dollars of market gain produced by investing with *Time In, Time Out*

$ Dow w/div = total Dow dollars, including dividends

$ TT w/div+int = total *TITO* dollars, including dividends and interest

Date	Action	Dow	$ Dow	$ TT	$ Dow w/ div	$TITO w/ div+int
10/28/53	Buy	273.3	100,000	100,000	100,000	100,000
5/5/54	Sell	317.9	116,319	116,319	119,432	119,432
10/28/54	Buy	355.7	130,150	116,319	137,194	120,291
5/5/55	Sell	423.4	154,921	138,458	167,333	146,716
10/28/55	Buy	453.8	166,045	138,458	183,629	148,068
5/4/56	Sell	516.4	188,950	157,558	213,680	172,300

Date	Action	Dow	$ Dow	$ TT	$ Dow w/ div	$TITO w/ div+int
10/29/56	Buy	486.1	177,863	157,558	205,952	174,635
5/3/57	Sell	497.5	182,034	161,253	215,555	182,778
10/28/57	Buy	435.2	159,239	161,253	193,034	185,565
5/5/58	Sell	461.1	168,716	170,849	209,043	200,955
10/28/58	Buy	535	195,756	170,849	247,147	202,697
5/5/59	Sell	625.9	229,016	199,878	294,167	241,260
10/28/59	Buy	642.2	234,980	199,878	306,840	245,357
5/5/60	Sell	608.3	222,576	189,327	295,906	236,614
10/28/60	Buy	581	212,587	189,327	287,074	240,416
5/5/61	Sell	690.7	252,726	225,074	346,506	290,188
10/30/61	Buy	698.7	255,653	225,074	356,645	294,362
5/4/62	Sell	671.2	245,591	216,215	348,842	287,921
10/29/62	Buy	569	208,196	216,215	301,056	292,063
5/3/63	Sell	718.1	262,752	272,872	385,354	373,843
10/28/63	Buy	755.6	276,473	272,872	412,110	379,733
5/5/64	Sell	826.6	302,452	298,513	459,278	423,195
10/28/64	Buy	876	320,527	298,513	495,718	430,277
5/5/65	Sell	932.2	341,090	317,664	536,682	465,834
10/28/65	Buy	959.5	351,079	317,664	560,820	474,768
5/5/66	Sell	899.8	329,235	297,899	535,514	453,344
10/28/66	Buy	809.6	296,231	297,899	490,279	463,125
5/5/67	Sell	906	331,504	333,370	557,963	527,060
10/30/67	Buy	888.2	324,991	333,370	557,249	537,168
5/3/68	Sell	919.2	336,334	345,005	587,142	565,984
10/28/68	Buy	961.3	351,738	345,005	623,755	580,641
5/5/69	Sell	959	350,896	344,180	633,771	589,965
10/28/69	Buy	860.3	314,782	344,180	579,459	606,937
5/5/70	Sell	709.7	259,678	283,929	489,546	512,761
10/28/70	Buy	754.5	276,070	283,929	529,696	527,511
5/5/71	Sell	940	343,944	353,736	670,316	667,551
10/28/71	Buy	836.4	306,037	353,736	608,261	683,225

Date	Action	Dow	$ Dow	$ TT	$ Dow w/ div	$TITO w/ div+int
5/5/72	Sell	941.2	344,383	398,058	696,050	781,834
10/30/72	Buy	946.4	346,286	398,058	711,960	798,656
5/4/73	Sell	953.9	349,030	401,213	730,631	819,601
10/29/73	Buy	987.1	361,178	401,213	768,194	846,570
5/3/74	Sell	845.9	309,513	343,821	674,708	743,547
10/28/74	Buy	636.2	232,784	343,821	521,788	772,066
5/5/75	Sell	855.6	313,063	462,391	716,714	1,060,489
10/28/75	Buy	838.5	306,806	462,391	723,278	1,090,944
5/5/76	Sell	986.5	360,959	544,006	870,864	1,313,552
10/28/76	Buy	956.1	349,835	544,006	864,251	1,348,096
5/5/77	Sell	943.4	345,188	536,780	873,730	1,362,882
10/28/77	Buy	818.6	299,524	536,780	777,261	1,398,075
5/5/78	Sell	829.1	303,366	543,665	809,085	1,455,318
10/30/78	Buy	806.1	294,951	543,665	809,285	1,506,327
5/4/79	Sell	847.5	310,099	571,587	876,813	1,632,017
10/29/79	Buy	809.3	296,121	571,587	863,914	1,711,414
5/5/80	Sell	816.3	298,683	576,531	900,405	1,783,703
10/28/80	Buy	931.7	340,907	576,531	1,055,598	1,881,709
5/5/81	Sell	972.4	355,799	601,716	1,134,944	2,023,150
10/28/81	Buy	838.4	306,769	601,716	1,010,280	2,158,951
5/5/82	Sell	854.5	312,660	613,271	1,061,580	2,268,580
10/28/82	Buy	1006	368,240	613,271	1,281,785	2,387,433
5/5/83	Sell	1219	446,286	743,249	1,591,202	2,963,748
10/28/83	Buy	1242	454,482	743,249	1,661,488	3,084,531
5/4/84	Sell	1165	426,381	697,294	1,602,236	2,974,531
10/29/84	Buy	1205	440,907	697,294	1,693,725	3,102,533
5/3/85	Sell	1247	456,348	721,714	1,797,227	3,292,127
10/28/85	Buy	1356	496,341	721,714	1,998,846	3,410,795
5/5/86	Sell	1793	656,348	954,375	2,691,117	4,592,074
10/28/86	Buy	1841	673,911	954,375	2,819,054	4,723,810
5/5/87	Sell	2338	855,507	1,211,545	3,636,705	6,093,925

Date	Action	Dow	$ Dow	$ TT	$ Dow w/ div	$TITO w/ div+int
10/28/87	Buy	1846	675,631	1,211,545	2,937,545	6,259,095
5/5/88	Sell	2020	739,188	1,325,515	3,275,008	6,978,134
10/28/88	Buy	2140	783,315	1,325,515	3,534,749	7,186,238
5/5/89	Sell	2382	871,570	1,474,859	4,016,249	8,165,140
10/30/89	Buy	2596	950,128	1,474,859	4,469,711	8,439,176
5/4/90	Sell	2710	991,731	1,539,437	4,760,885	8,988,935
10/29/90	Buy	2436	891,365	1,539,437	4,365,045	9,290,619
5/3/91	Sell	2938	1,075,338	1,857,170	5,349,274	11,385,464
10/28/91	Buy	3004	1,099,488	1,857,170	5,562,093	11,678,463
5/5/92	Sell	3359	1,229,199	2,076,268	6,314,935	13,259,169
10/28/92	Buy	3235	1,183,937	2,076,268	6,178,379	13,459,293
5/5/93	Sell	3449	1,262,020	2,213,201	6,684,608	14,562,088
10/28/93	Buy	3664	1,340,907	2,213,201	7,199,213	14,771,542
5/5/94	Sell	3696	1,352,360	2,232,104	7,368,798	15,119,501
10/28/94	Buy	3875	1,417,892	2,232,104	7,825,310	15,384,210
5/5/95	Sell	4343	1,589,243	2,501,851	8,891,673	17,480,631
10/30/95	Buy	4741	1,735,016	2,501,851	9,836,857	17,920,640
5/3/96	Sell	5478	2,004,391	2,890,282	11,504,140	20,958,073
10/28/96	Buy	6007	2,197,951	2,890,282	12,756,041	21,459,120
5/5/97	Sell	7213	2,639,480	3,470,888	15,468,765	26,022,657
10/28/97	Buy	7161	2,620,271	3,470,888	15,512,723	26,646,488
5/5/98	Sell	9147	3,347,091	4,433,656	19,975,532	34,312,337
10/28/98	Buy	8366	3,061,105	4,433,656	18,451,786	35,128,561
5/5/99	Sell	10955	4,008,562	5,805,937	24,341,664	46,341,728

Appendix B: Aggressive Time In Exit Date

The following table shows the returns dating back to 1953, produced by using the July 19th *Time In, Time Out* exit date for aggressive investors.

Table Headings

Date = calendar day of portfolio transaction, in month/day/year format

Action = either buying or selling the market index

Dow = Dow Jones index level

Dow $ Cum = total dollars of market gain produced by investing with buy and hold in the Dow Jones index

$TT = total dollars of market gain produced by investing with *Time In, Time Out*

$ Dow w/div = total Dow dollars, including dividends

$ TT w/div+int = total *TITO* dollars, including dividends and interest

Date	Action	Dow	Dow$ Cum	$TT	$Dow w/div	$TT w/div+int
10/28/53	Buy	273	100,000	100,000	100,000	100,000
7/19/54	Sell	339	123,893	123,893	128,284	128,284
10/28/54	Buy	356	130,150	123,893	136,948	128,811
7/19/55	Sell	457	167,106	159,072	181,356	170,580
10/28/55	Buy	454	166,045	159,072	182,855	171,535
7/19/56	Sell	514	188,035	180,139	213,537	200,317
10/29/56	Buy	486	177,863	180,139	204,732	201,897
7/19/57	Sell	516	188,694	191,109	223,764	220,665
10/28/57	Buy	435	159,239	191,109	191,487	222,661

Date	Action	Dow	Dow$ Cum	$TT	$Dow w/div	$TT w/div+int
7/18/58	Sell	487	178,046	213,680	220,395	256,275
10/28/58	Buy	535	195,756	213,680	245,088	257,572
7/17/59	Sell	657	240,432	262,447	307,799	323,477
10/28/59	Buy	642	234,980	262,447	303,816	326,760
7/19/60	Sell	625	228,613	255,336	302,753	325,617
10/28/60	Buy	581	212,587	255,336	284,130	328,366
7/19/61	Sell	683	249,799	300,031	341,192	394,312
10/30/61	Buy	699	255,653	300,031	352,636	397,553
7/19/62	Sell	573	209,733	246,139	297,769	335,698
10/29/62	Buy	569	208,196	246,139	298,187	338,457
7/19/63	Sell	694	253,897	300,169	371,199	421,329
10/28/63	Buy	756	276,473	300,169	407,856	425,369
7/17/64	Sell	851	311,526	338,226	471,345	491,585
10/28/64	Buy	876	320,527	338,226	490,237	496,286
7/19/65	Sell	880	322,100	339,886	505,001	511,232
10/28/65	Buy	960	351,079	339,886	554,964	516,834
7/19/66	Sell	884	323,491	313,177	524,593	488,550
10/28/66	Buy	810	296,231	313,177	485,116	494,573
7/19/67	Sell	903	330,516	349,423	554,287	565,093
10/30/67	Buy	888	324,991	349,423	550,839	571,286
7/19/68	Sell	914	334,394	359,534	581,011	602,577
10/28/68	Buy	961	351,738	359,534	616,642	611,334
7/18/69	Sell	846	309,513	316,373	558,545	553,737
10/28/69	Buy	860	314,782	316,373	573,551	562,840
7/17/70	Sell	735	268,972	270,331	506,132	496,680
10/28/70	Buy	755	276,070	270,331	524,952	504,845
7/19/71	Sell	886	324,332	317,590	630,988	606,819
10/28/71	Buy	836	306,037	317,590	601,754	615,131
7/19/72	Sell	917	335,419	348,081	675,448	690,464
10/30/72	Buy	946	346,286	348,081	704,022	698,953
7/19/73	Sell	907	331,760	333,479	692,383	687,398
10/29/73	Buy	987	361,178	333,479	760,349	701,196
7/19/74	Sell	788	288,291	266,182	630,068	581,051
10/28/74	Buy	636	232,784	266,182	516,409	593,786
7/18/75	Sell	862	315,551	360,823	721,296	829,371
10/28/75	Buy	839	306,806	360,823	713,319	843,005
7/19/76	Sell	991	362,532	426,360	869,630	1,027,734
10/28/76	Buy	956	349,835	426,360	850,713	1,043,178
7/19/77	Sell	919	336,370	409,950	846,577	1,038,106
10/28/77	Buy	819	299,524	409,950	764,425	1,053,613

Date	Action	Dow	Dow$ Cum	$TT	$Dow w/div	$TT w/div+int
7/19/78	Sell	841	307,611	421,017	815,726	1,124,320
10/30/78	Buy	806	294,951	421,017	795,200	1,147,588
7/19/79	Sell	827	302,708	432,090	851,973	1,229,520
10/29/79	Buy	809	296,121	432,090	848,219	1,264,649
7/18/80	Sell	924	338,090	493,329	1,008,191	1,503,160
10/28/80	Buy	932	340,907	493,329	1,034,446	1,546,002
7/17/81	Sell	959	350,860	507,731	1,109,609	1,658,335
10/28/81	Buy	838	306,769	507,731	987,900	1,721,943
7/19/82	Sell	826	302,269	500,282	1,017,160	1,772,945
10/28/82	Buy	1006	368,240	500,282	1,256,402	1,820,931
7/19/83	Sell	1197	438,017	595,079	1,545,374	2,239,744
10/28/83	Buy	1242	454,482	595,079	1,626,255	2,291,902
7/19/84	Sell	1103	403,549	528,390	1,502,613	2,117,653
10/29/84	Buy	1205	440,907	528,390	1,661,493	2,169,726
7/19/85	Sell	1360	497,439	596,138	1,935,348	2,527,350
10/28/85	Buy	1357	496,341	596,138	1,958,224	2,579,282
7/18/86	Sell	1778	650,567	781,374	2,631,058	3,465,508
10/28/86	Buy	1842	673,911	781,374	2,756,713	3,518,909
7/17/87	Sell	2510	918,405	1,064,854	3,834,845	4,895,132
10/28/87	Buy	1847	675,631	1,064,854	2,860,588	4,972,006
7/19/88	Sell	2097	767,398	1,209,487	3,332,697	5,792,582
10/28/88	Buy	2141	783,315	1,209,487	3,439,172	5,893,111
7/19/89	Sell	2584	945,628	1,460,107	4,266,371	7,310,538
10/30/89	Buy	2597	950,128	1,460,107	4,342,193	7,450,741
7/19/90	Sell	2994	1,095,426	1,683,394	5,132,567	8,806,937
10/29/90	Buy	2436	891,365	1,683,394	4,229,411	8,975,837
7/19/91	Sell	3016	1,103,659	2,084,324	5,348,842	11,351,541
10/28/91	Buy	3005	1,099,488	2,084,324	5,381,586	11,514,606
7/17/92	Sell	3332	1,219,027	2,310,937	6,095,260	13,041,603
10/28/92	Buy	3236	1,183,937	2,310,937	5,972,742	13,148,502
7/19/93	Sell	3535	1,293,560	2,524,911	6,658,288	14,657,677
10/28/93	Buy	3665	1,340,907	2,524,911	6,957,069	14,778,151
7/19/94	Sell	3748	1,371,497	2,582,510	7,260,471	15,422,635
10/28/94	Buy	3875	1,417,892	2,582,510	7,562,069	15,584,571
7/19/95	Sell	4629	1,693,707	3,084,870	9,196,933	18,953,842
10/30/95	Buy	4742	1,735,016	3,084,870	9,497,843	19,226,465
7/19/96	Sell	5427	1,985,657	3,530,510	11,054,991	22,378,597
10/28/96	Buy	6007	2,197,951	3,530,510	12,314,330	22,684,315
7/18/97	Sell	7891	2,887,120	4,637,505	16,373,963	30,162,594
10/28/97	Buy	7161	2,620,271	4,637,505	14,955,241	30,575,780

Date	Action	Dow	Dow$ Cum	$TT	$Dow w/div	$TT w/div+int
7/17/98	Sell	9338	3,416,758	6,047,174	19,714,022	40,305,041
10/28/98	Buy	8366	3,061,105	6,047,174	17,765,191	40,849,081
7/19/99	Sell	11188	4,093,560	8,086,776	23,996,195	55,176,582

Appendix C: Conservative Time Out Period

Here, we assume that you sold the index on May 5th and invested in money market fund or treasury bills from May 6th until October 27th. The following table summarizes how the market performed while you were not invested.

Table Headings

Date = calendar day of portfolio transaction, in month/day/year format

Action = either buying or selling the market index

Dow = Dow Jones index level

Period% = performance of market returns during the Time Out period

Dow % Cum = cumulative gain of the Dow Jones index

%Time Out = cumulative return during the Time Out period

$ Dow = cumulative return in dollars of the Dow Jones index

$ Time Out = cumulative return in dollars of the Time Out period

Date	Action	Dow	Period%	Dow% cum	%Time Out	Dow$	$Time Out
5/6/53	Buy	278.2	0.00%	0.00%	0.00%	100,000	100,000
10/27/53	Sell	273.3	-1.76%	-1.76%	-1.76%	98,239	98,239
5/6/54	Buy	317.9	16.32%	14.27%	-1.76%	114,270	98,239
10/27/54	Sell	355.7	11.89%	27.86%	9.92%	127,858	109,920
5/6/55	Buy	423.4	19.03%	52.19%	9.92%	152,193	109,920
10/27/55	Sell	453.8	7.18%	63.12%	17.81%	163,120	117,812
5/7/56	Buy	516.4	13.79%	85.62%	17.81%	185,622	117,812
10/26/56	Sell	486.1	-5.87%	74.73%	10.90%	174,730	110,899
5/6/57	Buy	497.5	2.35%	78.83%	10.90%	178,828	110,899

Date	Action	Dow	Period%	Dow% cum	%Time Out	Dow$	$Time Out
10/25/57	Sell	435.2	-12.52%	56.43%	-2.99%	156,434	97,012
5/6/58	Buy	461.1	5.95%	65.74%	-2.99%	165,744	97,012
10/27/58	Sell	535	16.03%	92.31%	12.56%	192,308	112,560
5/6/59	Buy	625.9	16.99%	124.98%	12.56%	224,982	112,560
10/27/59	Sell	642.2	2.60%	130.84%	15.49%	230,841	115,491
5/6/60	Buy	608.3	-5.28%	118.66%	15.49%	218,656	115,491
10/27/60	Sell	581	-4.49%	108.84%	10.31%	208,843	110,308
5/8/61	Buy	690.7	18.88%	148.27%	10.31%	248,275	110,308
10/27/61	Sell	698.7	1.16%	151.15%	11.59%	251,150	111,586
5/7/62	Buy	671.2	-3.94%	141.27%	11.59%	241,265	111,586
10/26/62	Sell	569	-15.23%	104.53%	-5.40%	204,529	94,595
5/6/63	Buy	718.1	26.20%	158.12%	-5.40%	258,124	94,595
10/25/63	Sell	755.6	5.22%	171.60%	-0.47%	271,603	99,535
5/6/64	Buy	826.6	9.40%	197.12%	-0.47%	297,124	99,535
10/27/64	Sell	876	5.98%	214.88%	5.48%	314,881	105,483
5/6/65	Buy	932.2	6.42%	235.08%	5.48%	335,083	105,483
10/27/65	Sell	959.5	2.93%	244.90%	8.57%	344,896	108,573
5/6/66	Buy	899.8	-6.22%	223.44%	8.57%	323,436	108,573
10/27/66	Sell	809.6	-10.02%	191.01%	-2.31%	291,014	97,689
5/8/67	Buy	906	11.91%	225.66%	-2.31%	325,665	97,689
10/27/67	Sell	888.2	-1.96%	219.27%	-4.23%	319,267	95,770
5/6/68	Buy	919.2	3.49%	230.41%	-4.23%	330,410	95,770
10/25/68	Sell	961.3	4.58%	245.54%	0.16%	345,543	100,156
5/6/69	Buy	959	-0.24%	244.72%	0.16%	344,716	100,156
10/27/69	Sell	860.3	-10.29%	209.24%	-10.15%	309,238	89,848
5/6/70	Buy	709.7	-17.51%	155.10%	-10.15%	255,104	89,848
10/27/70	Sell	754.5	6.31%	171.21%	-4.48%	271,208	95,519
5/6/71	Buy	940	24.59%	237.89%	-4.48%	337,886	95,519
10/27/71	Sell	836.4	-11.02%	200.65%	-15.01%	300,647	84,992
5/8/72	Buy	941.2	12.53%	238.32%	-15.01%	338,318	84,992
10/27/72	Sell	946.4	0.55%	240.19%	-14.54%	340,187	85,462
5/7/73	Buy	953.9	0.79%	242.88%	-14.54%	342,883	85,462
10/26/73	Sell	987.1	3.48%	254.82%	-11.56%	354,817	88,436
5/6/74	Buy	845.9	-14.30%	204.06%	-11.56%	304,062	88,436
10/25/74	Sell	636.2	-24.79%	128.68%	-33.49%	228,684	66,513
5/6/75	Buy	855.6	34.49%	207.55%	-33.49%	307,549	66,513
10/27/75	Sell	838.5	-2.00%	201.40%	-34.82%	301,402	65,183
5/6/76	Buy	986.5	17.65%	254.60%	-34.82%	354,601	65,183
10/27/76	Sell	956.1	-3.08%	243.67%	-36.83%	343,674	63,175
5/6/77	Buy	943.4	-1.33%	239.11%	-36.83%	339,109	63,175

Date	Action	Dow	Period%	Dow% cum	%Time Out	Dow$	$Time Out
10/27/77	Sell	818.6	-13.23%	194.25%	-45.18%	294,249	54,817
5/8/78	Buy	829.1	1.28%	198.02%	-45.18%	298,023	54,817
10/27/78	Sell	806.1	-2.77%	189.76%	-46.70%	289,756	53,297
5/7/79	Buy	847.5	5.14%	204.64%	-46.70%	304,637	53,297
10/26/79	Sell	809.3	-4.51%	190.91%	-49.11%	290,906	50,894
5/6/80	Buy	816.3	0.86%	193.42%	-49.11%	293,422	50,894
10/27/80	Sell	931.7	14.14%	234.90%	-41.91%	334,903	58,089
5/6/81	Buy	972.4	4.37%	249.53%	-41.91%	349,533	58,089
10/27/81	Sell	838.4	-13.78%	201.37%	-49.92%	301,366	50,084
5/6/82	Buy	854.5	1.92%	207.15%	-49.92%	307,153	50,084
10/27/82	Sell	1006.4	17.78%	261.75%	-41.01%	361,754	58,988
5/6/83	Buy	1219.7	21.19%	338.43%	-41.01%	438,426	58,988
10/27/83	Sell	1242.1	1.84%	346.48%	-39.93%	446,477	60,071
5/7/84	Buy	1165.3	-6.18%	318.87%	-39.93%	418,871	60,071
10/26/84	Sell	1205	3.41%	333.14%	-37.88%	433,142	62,118
5/6/85	Buy	1247.2	3.50%	348.31%	-37.88%	448,311	62,118
10/25/85	Sell	1356.5	8.76%	387.60%	-32.44%	487,599	67,561
5/6/86	Buy	1793.8	32.24%	544.79%	-32.44%	644,788	67,561
10/27/86	Sell	1841.8	2.68%	562.04%	-30.63%	662,042	69,369
5/6/87	Buy	2338.1	26.95%	740.44%	-30.63%	840,439	69,369
10/27/87	Sell	1846.5	-21.03%	563.73%	-45.22%	663,731	54,784
5/6/88	Buy	2020.2	9.41%	626.17%	-45.22%	726,168	54,784
10/27/88	Sell	2140.8	5.97%	669.52%	-41.95%	769,518	58,054
5/8/89	Buy	2382	11.27%	756.22%	-41.95%	856,219	58,054
10/27/89	Sell	2596.7	9.01%	833.39%	-36.71%	933,393	63,287
5/7/90	Buy	2710.4	4.38%	874.26%	-36.71%	974,263	63,287
10/26/90	Sell	2436.1	-10.12%	775.66%	-43.12%	875,665	56,882
5/6/91	Buy	2938.9	20.64%	956.40%	-43.12%	1,056,398	56,882
10/25/91	Sell	3004.9	2.25%	980.12%	-41.84%	1,080,122	58,160
5/6/92	Buy	3359.4	11.80%	1107.55%	-41.84%	1,207,549	58,160
10/27/92	Sell	3235.7	-3.68%	1063.08%	-43.98%	1,163,084	56,018
5/6/93	Buy	3449.1	6.60%	1139.79%	-43.98%	1,239,792	56,018
10/27/93	Sell	3664.7	6.25%	1217.29%	-40.48%	1,317,290	59,520
5/6/94	Buy	3696	0.85%	1228.54%	-40.48%	1,328,541	59,520
10/27/94	Sell	3875.1	4.85%	1292.92%	-37.60%	1,392,919	62,404
5/8/95	Buy	4343.4	12.08%	1461.25%	-37.60%	1,561,251	62,404
10/27/95	Sell	4741.8	9.17%	1604.46%	-31.87%	1,704,457	68,128
5/6/96	Buy	5478	15.53%	1869.09%	-31.87%	1,969,087	68,128
10/25/96	Sell	6007	9.66%	2059.24%	-25.29%	2,159,238	74,707
5/6/97	Buy	7213.7	20.09%	2492.99%	-25.29%	2,592,991	74,707

Date	Action	Dow	Period%	Dow% cum	%Time Out	Dow$	$Time Out
10/27/97	Sell	7161.2	-0.73%	2474.12%	-25.84%	2,574,119	74,163
5/6/98	Buy	9147.6	27.74%	3188.14%	-25.84%	3,288,138	74,163
10/27/98	Sell	8366	-8.54%	2907.19%	-32.17%	3,007,189	67,826
5/6/99	Buy	10955.4	30.95%	3837.96%	-32.17%	3,937,958	67,826
10/27/99	Sell	10394.8	5.12%	3636.48%	-35.64%	3,736,481	64,356

Appendix D: Aggressive Time Out Period

The following table shows the effect of investing in the market from July 20th to October 27th every year since 1953. Comparisons can be made to the previous example for May 5th. July 19th provided even greater losses.

Table Headings

Date = calendar day of portfolio transaction, in month/day/year format

Action = either buying or selling the market index

Dow = Dow Jones index level

Period% = performance of market returns during the Time Out period

Dow % Cum = cumulative gain of the Dow Jones index

%Time Out = cumulative return during the Time Out period

$ Dow cum = cumulative return in dollars of the Dow Jones index

$ Time Out cum = cumulative return in dollars of the Time Out period

Date	Action	Dow	Period%	Dow% cum	%Time Out	$ Dow cum	$Time Out cum
7/20/53	Buy	271	0.00%	0.00%	0.00%	100,000	100,000
10/27/53	Sell	273	0.81%	0.81%	0.81%	100,812	100,812
7/20/54	Buy	339	23.89%	24.90%	0.81%	124,899	100,812
10/27/54	Sell	356	5.05%	31.21%	5.90%	131,206	105,903
7/20/55	Buy	457	28.39%	68.46%	5.90%	168,462	105,903
10/27/55	Sell	454	-0.63%	67.39%	5.23%	167,392	105,230
7/20/56	Buy	514	13.24%	89.56%	5.23%	189,561	105,230
10/26/56	Sell	486	-5.41%	79.31%	-0.46%	179,307	99,538
7/22/57	Buy	516	6.09%	90.23%	-0.46%	190,225	99,538
10/25/57	Sell	435	-15.61%	60.53%	-16.00%	160,531	84,000
7/21/58	Buy	487	11.81%	79.49%	-16.00%	179,491	84,000
10/27/58	Sell	535	9.95%	97.34%	-7.64%	197,344	92,355
7/20/59	Buy	657	22.82%	142.38%	-7.64%	242,383	92,355
10/27/59	Sell	642	-2.27%	136.89%	-9.74%	236,887	90,261

Date	Action	Dow	Period%	Dow% cum	%Time Out	$ Dow cum	$Time Out cum
7/20/60	Buy	625	-2.71%	130.47%	-9.74%	230,468	90,261
10/27/60	Sell	581	-7.01%	114.31%	-16.07%	214,312	83,933
7/20/61	Buy	683	17.50%	151.83%	-16.07%	251,826	83,933
10/27/61	Sell	699	2.34%	157.73%	-14.10%	257,728	85,901
7/20/62	Buy	573	-17.96%	111.43%	-14.10%	211,435	85,901
10/26/62	Sell	569	-0.73%	109.89%	-14.73%	209,886	85,271
7/22/63	Buy	694	21.95%	155.96%	-14.73%	255,957	85,271
10/25/63	Sell	756	8.89%	178.72%	-7.15%	278,716	92,853
7/20/64	Buy	851	12.68%	214.05%	-7.15%	314,054	92,853
10/27/64	Sell	876	2.89%	223.13%	-4.46%	323,128	95,536
7/20/65	Buy	880	0.49%	224.71%	-4.46%	324,714	95,536
10/27/65	Sell	960	9.00%	253.93%	4.13%	353,928	104,131
7/20/66	Buy	884	-7.86%	226.12%	4.13%	326,116	104,131
10/27/66	Sell	810	-8.43%	198.64%	-4.64%	298,635	95,357
7/20/67	Buy	903	11.57%	233.20%	-4.64%	333,198	95,357
10/27/67	Sell	888	-1.67%	227.63%	-6.24%	327,628	93,763
7/22/68	Buy	914	2.89%	237.11%	-6.24%	337,108	93,763
10/25/68	Sell	961	5.19%	254.59%	-1.37%	354,592	98,626
7/22/69	Buy	846	-12.00%	212.03%	-1.37%	312,025	98,626
10/27/69	Sell	860	1.70%	217.34%	0.30%	317,337	100,305
7/20/70	Buy	735	-14.55%	171.15%	0.30%	271,155	100,305
10/27/70	Sell	755	2.64%	178.31%	2.95%	278,311	102,952
7/20/71	Buy	886	17.48%	226.96%	2.95%	326,964	102,952
10/27/71	Sell	836	-5.64%	208.52%	-2.86%	308,521	97,144
7/20/72	Buy	917	9.60%	238.14%	-2.86%	338,141	97,144
10/27/72	Sell	946	3.24%	249.10%	0.29%	349,096	100,292
7/20/73	Buy	907	-4.19%	234.45%	0.29%	334,452	100,292
10/26/73	Sell	987	8.87%	264.11%	9.18%	364,109	109,185
7/22/74	Buy	788	-20.18%	190.63%	9.18%	290,631	109,185
10/25/74	Sell	636	-19.25%	134.67%	-11.84%	234,674	88,163
7/21/75	Buy	862	35.55%	218.11%	-11.84%	318,111	88,163
10/27/75	Sell	839	-2.77%	209.30%	-14.28%	309,295	85,720
7/20/76	Buy	991	18.16%	265.47%	-14.28%	365,474	85,720
10/27/76	Sell	956	-3.50%	252.67%	-17.28%	352,674	82,717
7/20/77	Buy	919	-3.85%	239.10%	-17.28%	339,100	82,717
10/27/77	Sell	819	-10.95%	201.95%	-26.34%	301,955	73,657
7/20/78	Buy	841	2.70%	210.11%	-26.34%	310,107	73,657
10/27/78	Sell	806	-4.12%	197.34%	-29.37%	297,344	70,625
7/20/79	Buy	827	2.63%	205.16%	-29.37%	305,164	70,625
10/26/79	Sell	809	-2.18%	198.52%	-30.91%	298,525	69,089

Date	Action	Dow	Period%	Dow% cum	%Time Out	$ Dow cum	$Time Out cum
7/21/80	Buy	924	14.17%	240.83%	-30.91%	340,834	69,089
10/27/80	Sell	932	0.83%	243.67%	-30.34%	343,674	69,664
7/20/81	Buy	959	2.92%	253.71%	-30.34%	353,707	69,664
10/27/81	Sell	838	-12.57%	209.26%	-39.09%	309,259	60,910
7/20/82	Buy	826	-1.47%	204.72%	-39.09%	304,722	60,910
10/27/82	Sell	1006	21.83%	271.23%	-25.80%	371,228	74,204
7/20/83	Buy	1197	18.95%	341.57%	-25.80%	441,571	74,204
10/27/83	Sell	1242	3.76%	358.17%	-23.01%	458,170	76,993
7/20/84	Buy	1103	-11.21%	306.82%	-23.01%	406,824	76,993
10/26/84	Sell	1205	9.26%	344.49%	-15.88%	444,485	84,121
7/22/85	Buy	1360	12.82%	401.48%	-15.88%	501,475	84,121
10/25/85	Sell	1357	-0.22%	400.37%	-16.06%	500,369	83,935
7/21/86	Buy	1778	31.07%	555.85%	-16.06%	655,847	83,935
10/27/86	Sell	1842	3.59%	579.38%	-13.05%	679,380	86,947
7/1/87	Buy	2510	36.28%	825.86%	-13.05%	925,858	86,947
10/27/87	Sell	1847	-26.43%	581.11%	-36.04%	681,114	63,963
7/20/88	Buy	2097	13.58%	673.63%	-36.04%	773,626	63,963
10/27/88	Sell	2141	2.07%	689.67%	-34.71%	789,672	65,290
7/20/89	Buy	2584	20.72%	853.30%	-34.71%	953,301	65,290
10/27/89	Sell	2597	0.48%	857.84%	-34.40%	957,838	65,601
7/20/90	Buy	2994	15.29%	1004.32%	-34.40%	1,104,316	65,601
10/26/90	Sell	2436	-18.63%	798.60%	-46.62%	898,598	53,380
7/22/91	Buy	3016	23.82%	1012.62%	-46.62%	1,112,615	53,380
10/25/91	Sell	3005	-0.38%	1008.41%	-46.82%	1,108,410	53,178
7/20/92	Buy	3332	10.87%	1128.92%	-46.82%	1,228,919	53,178
10/27/92	Sell	3236	-2.88%	1093.54%	-48.35%	1,193,545	51,648
7/20/93	Buy	3535	9.26%	1204.06%	-48.35%	1,304,058	51,648
10/27/93	Sell	3665	3.66%	1251.79%	-46.46%	1,351,789	53,538
7/20/94	Buy	3748	2.28%	1282.63%	-46.46%	1,382,626	53,538
10/27/94	Sell	3875	3.38%	1329.40%	-44.65%	1,429,399	55,349
7/20/95	Buy	4629	19.45%	1607.45%	-44.65%	1,707,451	55,349
10/27/95	Sell	4742	2.44%	1649.10%	-43.30%	1,749,096	56,699
7/22/96	Buy	5427	14.45%	1901.77%	-43.30%	2,001,771	56,699
10/25/96	Sell	6007	10.69%	2115.79%	-37.24%	2,215,788	62,761
7/21/97	Buy	7891	31.36%	2810.55%	-37.24%	2,910,550	62,761
10/27/97	Sell	7161	-9.24%	2541.53%	-43.04%	2,641,534	56,960
7/20/98	Buy	9338	30.40%	3344.49%	-43.04%	3,444,485	56,960
10/27/98	Sell	8366	-10.41%	2985.95%	-48.97%	3,085,946	51,031
7/20/99	Buy	11188	33.73%	4026.78%	-48.97%	4,126,780	51,031
10/27/99	Sell	10395	-7.09%	3734.34%	-52.59%	3,834,338	47,415

Appendix E: The Best and Worst Days

The following tables detail the best and worst days for the Dow of the last ten years.

Best Dates for 1990	Day 1	Day 2	Day 3	Day 4	Day 5	Day 6	Day 7	Day 8	Day 9	Day 10	Average
	8/27/90	10/19/90	10/18/90	10/1/90	5/11/90	11/12/90	1/2/90	8/24/90	1/31/90	11/9/90	
	3.11%	2.78%	2.71%	2.58%	2.30%	2.08%	2.07%	1.99%	1.86%	1.83%	1.83%

Worst Dates for 1990	Day 1	Day 2	Day 3	Day 4	Day 5	Day 6	Day 7	Day 8	Day 9	Day 10	Average
	8/6/90	10/9/90	8/23/90	1/22/90	1/12/90	8/16/90	9/24/90	8/21/90	10/26/90	8/3/90	
	-3.32%	-3.10%	-3.00%	-2.89%	-2.59%	-2.43%	-2.36%	-1.97%	-1.94%	-1.92%	-2.55%

Best Dates for 1991	Day 1	Day 2	Day 3	Day 4	Day 5	Day 6	Day 7	Day 8	Day 9	Day 10	Average
	1/17/91	8/21/91	12/23/91	2/11/91	4/2/91	12/30/91	3/5/91	2/15/91	1/30/91	4/16/91	
	4.57%	3.02%	3.00%	2.53%	2.22%	2.01%	2.00%	2.00%	1.90%	1.83%	2.51%

Worst Dates for 1991	Day 1	Day 2	Day 3	Day 4	Day 5	Day 6	Day 7	Day 8	Day 9	Day 10	Average
	11/15/91	8/19/91	3/19/91	6/24/91	5/10/91	1/7/91	4/9/91	1/9/91	1/3/91	11/19/91	
	-3.93%	-2.36%	-2.12%	-1.77%	-1.72%	-1.69%	-1.56%	-1.56%	-1.42%	-1.38%	-1.95%

Best Dates for 1992	Day 1	Day 2	Day 3	Day 4	Day 5	Day 6	Day 7	Day 8	Day 9	Day 10	Average
	9/14/92	1/14/92	7/28/92	2/20/92	4/15/92	4/9/92	7/29/92	12/18/92	5/4/92	10/12/92	
	2.13%	1.90%	1.58%	1.56%	1.44%	1.37%	1.35%	1.35%	1.26%	1.21%	1.52%

Worst Dates for 1992	Day 1	Day 2	Day 3	Day 4	Day 5	Day 6	Day 7	Day 8	Day 9	Day 10	Average
	4/7/92	10/2/92	8/21/92	9/15/92	1/29/92	7/7/92	6/17/92	10/9/92	9/22/92	9/25/92	
	-1.89%	-1.65%	-1.54%	-1.45%	-1.44%	-1.32%	-1.25%	-1.24%	-1.20%	-1.14%	-1.41%

Best Dates for 1993

	Day 1	Day 2	Day 3	Day 4	Day 5	Day 6	Day 7	Day 8	Day 9	Day 10	Average
	3/8/93	5/19/93	2/3/93	3/2/93	2/4/93	3/18/93	6/28/93	7/8/93	1/25/93	2/24/93	
	1.90%	1.61%	1.35%	1.34%	1.27%	1.14%	1.13%	1.11%	1.09%	1.00%	1.29%

Worst Dates for 1993

	Day 1	Day 2	Day 3	Day 4	Day 5	Day 6	Day 7	Day 8	Day 9	Day 10	Average
	2/16/93	4/2/93	1/7/93	9/21/93	9/20/93	11/4/93	5/13/93	7/6/93	11/3/93	2/12/93	
	-2.44%	-1.99%	-1.10%	-1.08%	-1.04%	-1.01%	-0.98%	-0.98%	-0.97%	-0.89%	-1.25%

Best Dates for 1994

	Day 1	Day 2	Day 3	Day 4	Day 5	Day 6	Day 7	Day 8	Day 9	Day 10	Average
	4/5/94	8/24/94	4/25/94	9/15/94	4/21/94	10/11/94	10/28/94	5/17/94	8/26/94	6/27/94	
	2.28%	1.88%	1.56%	1.50%	1.49%	1.45%	1.43%	1.34%	1.34%	1.34%	1.56%

Worst Dates for 1994

	Day 1	Day 2	Day 3	Day 4	Day 5	Day 6	Day 7	Day 8	Day 9	Day 10	Average
	11/22/94	2/4/94	3/30/94	9/20/94	3/29/94	6/24/94	12/8/94	2/24/94	3/24/94	3/25/94	
	-2.43%	-2.43%	-1.95%	-1.72%	-1.69%	-1.68%	-1.33%	-1.33%	-1.25%	-1.21%	-1.70%

Best Dates for 1995

	Day 1	Day 2	Day 3	Day 4	Day 5	Day 6	Day 7	Day 8	Day 9	Day 10	Average
	5/31/95	2/3/95	3/10/95	1/13/95	5/22/95	3/24/95	11/8/95	7/6/95	11/15/95	12/4/95	
	1.97%	1.49%	1.31%	1.28%	1.25%	1.25%	1.16%	1.06%	1.05%	1.03%	1.29%

Worst Dates for 1995

	Day 1	Day 2	Day 3	Day 4	Day 5	Day 6	Day 7	Day 8	Day 9	Day 10	Average
	12/18/95	5/18/95	7/19/95	1/19/95	7/18/95	10/26/95	12/20/95	5/26/95	10/9/95	3/7/95	
	-1.96%	-1.85%	-1.22%	-1.19%	-1.06%	-1.05%	-0.99%	-0.98%	-0.90%	-0.88%	-1.21%

Best Dates for 1996										
Day 1	Day 2	Day 3	Day 4	Day 5	Day 6	Day 7	Day 8	Day 9	Day 10	Average
3/11/96	12/19/96	3/18/96	2/22/96	7/18/96	11/6/96	8/2/96	1/30/96	7/1/96	9/9/96	
2.02%	2.00%	1.77%	1.68%	1.62%	1.59%	1.52%	1.44%	1.33%	1.31%	1.63%
Worst Dates for 1996										
Day 1	Day 2	Day 3	Day 4	Day 5	Day 6	Day 7	Day 8	Day 9	Day 10	Average
3/8/96	7/15/96	7/5/96	1/10/96	4/8/96	12/31/96	12/12/96	7/11/96	5/2/96	4/10/96	
-3.03%	-2.92%	-2.01%	-1.89%	-1.56%	-1.54%	-1.54%	-1.48%	-1.38%	-1.34%	-1.87%
Best Dates for 1997										
Day 1	Day 2	Day 3	Day 4	Day 5	Day 6	Day 7	Day 8	Day 9	Day 10	Average
10/28/97	9/2/97	11/3/97	4/29/97	4/22/97	12/1/97	9/16/97	4/15/97	6/24/97	5/5/97	
4.71%	3.38%	3.12%	2.64%	2.60%	2.43%	2.26%	2.10%	2.02%	2.02%	2.73%
Worst Dates for 1997										
Day 1	Day 2	Day 3	Day 4	Day 5	Day 6	Day 7	Day 8	Day 9	Day 10	Average
10/27/97	8/15/97	6/23/97	3/31/97	10/23/97	3/13/97	4/11/97	11/12/97	3/27/97	5/7/97	
-7.18%	-3.11%	-2.47%	-2.33%	-2.33%	-2.28%	-2.27%	-2.08%	-2.04%	-1.93%	-2.80%
Best Dates for 1998										
Day 1	Day 2	Day 3	Day 4	Day 5	Day 6	Day 7	Day 8	Day 9	Day 10	Average
9/8/98	10/15/98	9/1/98	9/23/98	2/2/98	9/11/98	11/23/98	10/9/98	10/2/98	9/14/98	
4.98%	4.15%	3.82%	3.26%	2.55%	2.36%	2.34%	2.17%	1.99%	1.92%	2.95%
Worst Dates for 1998										
Day 1	Day 2	Day 3	Day 4	Day 5	Day 6	Day 7	Day 8	Day 9	Day 10	Average
8/31/98	8/27/98	8/4/98	9/10/98	9/30/98	1/9/98	10/1/98	9/17/98	6/15/98	11/30/98	
-6.37%	-4.19%	-3.41%	-3.17%	-2.94%	-2.85%	-2.68%	-2.67%	-2.34%	-2.32%	-3.29%

Best Dates for 1999

	Day 1	Day 2	Day 3	Day 4	Day 5	Day 6	Day 7	Day 8	Day 9	Day 10	Average
	3/5/99	1/6/99	1/15/99	2/22/99	12/3/99	10/28/99	9/3/99	5/3/99	3/4/99	2/11/99	
	2.84%	2.51%	2.41%	2.28%	2.24%	2.19%	2.17%	2.09%	2.06%	2.03%	2.28%

Worst Dates for 1999

	Day 1	Day 2	Day 3	Day 4	Day 5	Day 6	Day 7	Day 8	Day 9	Day 10	Average
	10/15/99	1/14/99	3/23/99	5/27/99	10/12/99	9/21/99	9/23/99	10/13/99	5/14/99	7/20/99	
	-2.59%	-2.45%	-2.21%	-2.20%	-2.17%	-2.08%	-1.95%	-1.77%	-1.75%	-1.71%	-2.09%

Averages Best Gains per Day

	Day 1	Day 2	Day 3	Day 4	Day 5	Day 6	Day 7	Day 8	Day 9	Day 10	Average
	3.05%	2.47%	2.26%	2.06%	1.90%	1.79%	1.74%	1.66%	1.59%	1.55%	2.01%

Average Worst Gains per Day

	Day 1	Day 2	Day 3	Day 4	Day 5	Day 6	Day 7	Day 8	Day 9	Day 10	Average
	-3.52%	-2.61%	-2.10%	-1.97%	-1.85%	-1.79%	-1.69%	-1.61%	-1.52%	-1.47%	-2.01%

Best Dates for Period

	Day 1	Day 2	Day 3	Day 4	Day 5	Day 6	Day 7	Day 8	Day 9	Day 10	Average
	9/8/98	10/28/97	1/17/91	10/15/98	9/1/98	9/2/97	9/23/98	11/3/97	8/27/90	8/21/91	
	4.98%	4.71%	4.57%	4.15%	3.82%	3.38%	3.26%	3.12%	3.11%	3.02%	3.81%

Worst Dates for Period

	Day 1	Day 2	Day 3	Day 4	Day 5	Day 6	Day 7	Day 8	Day 9	Day 10	Average
	10/27/97	8/31/98	8/27/98	11/15/91	8/4/98	8/6/90	9/10/98	8/15/97	10/9/90	3/8/96	
	-7.18%	-6.37%	-4.19%	-3.93%	-3.41%	-3.32%	-3.17%	-3.11%	-3.10%	-3.03%	-4.08%

Appendix F: Dow Jones Index Monthly Gains

The following table shows all of the monthly and the yearly percentage gains of the Dow Jones Index, dating from 1953 to 1999.

	Jan	Feb	Mar	Apr	May	Jun	Jul	Aug	Sep	Oct	Nov	Dec	Year
1953	-0.65	-1.97	-1.55	-1.82	-0.91	-1.47	2.65	-5.16	1.07	4.47	2.03	-0.18	-3.77
1954	4.09	0.72	3.06	5.21	2.57	1.83	4.32	-3.48	7.36	-2.33	9.86	4.55	43.97
1955	1.09	0.76	-0.53	3.91	-0.19	6.24	3.21	0.49	-0.34	-2.51	6.24	1.06	20.77
1956	-3.62	2.76	5.81	0.84	-7.36	3.07	5.07	-3.05	-5.32	0.97	-1.48	5.65	2.27
1957	-4.06	-3.05	2.20	4.13	2.12	-0.32	1.03	-4.74	-5.80	-3.35	2.02	-3.16	-12.77
1958	3.28	-2.24	1.57	2.04	1.49	3.35	5.19	1.11	4.62	2.09	2.63	4.70	33.97
1959	1.76	1.60	-0.30	3.67	3.21	-0.03	4.86	-1.56	-4.92	2.36	1.95	3.06	16.40
1960	-8.36	1.20	-2.14	-2.42	3.96	2.41	-3.73	1.51	-7.33	0.05	2.89	3.13	-9.35
1961	5.24	2.14	2.19	0.31	2.65	-1.82	3.13	2.06	-2.60	0.39	2.51	1.32	18.70
1962	-4.25	1.16	-0.16	-5.90	-7.80	-8.49	6.52	1.89	-4.96	1.87	10.09	0.43	-10.81
1963	4.72	-2.93	2.96	5.16	1.30	-2.76	-1.63	4.87	0.48	3.06	-0.62	1.67	17.01
1964	2.92	1.88	1.65	-0.31	1.21	1.33	1.15	-0.31	4.40	-0.26	0.26	-0.15	14.56
1965	3.29	0.07	-1.59	3.73	-0.47	-5.45	1.58	1.29	4.20	3.25	-1.47	2.39	10.89
1966	1.46	-3.21	-2.85	0.96	-5.31	-1.58	-2.61	-6.96	-1.80	4.25	-1.92	-0.75	-18.94
1967	8.17	-1.24	3.17	3.59	-4.96	0.90	5.10	-0.32	2.82	-5.07	-0.44	3.35	15.20
1968	-5.48	-1.75	0.02	8.50	-1.45	-0.13	-1.65	1.47	4.44	1.77	3.43	-4.19	4.28
1969	0.24	-4.32	3.35	1.57	-1.33	-6.87	-6.61	2.60	-2.82	5.28	-5.11	-1.46	-15.19
1970	-7.03	4.50	1.03	-6.30	-4.85	-2.41	7.40	4.15	-0.51	-0.67	5.10	5.64	4.81
1971	3.53	1.19	2.91	4.14	-3.61	-1.84	-3.67	4.62	-1.21	-5.43	-0.92	7.09	6.12
1972	1.35	2.87	1.36	1.44	0.68	-3.30	-0.46	4.22	-1.08	0.23	6.56	0.18	14.58
1973	-2.06	-4.39	-0.43	-3.11	-2.17	-1.08	3.89	-4.19	6.70	1.00	-14.04	3.48	-16.58
1974	0.55	0.57	-1.60	-1.17	-4.13	0.02	-5.61	-10.40	-10.42	9.48	-7.03	-0.40	-27.58
1975	14.20	5.03	3.94	6.91	1.34	5.61	-5.40	0.46	-4.96	5.30	2.95	-0.96	38.33
1976	14.42	-0.28	2.77	-0.26	-2.18	2.83	-1.81	-1.11	1.69	-2.56	-1.83	6.07	17.87
1977	-5.01	-1.89	-1.85	0.85	-3.04	1.96	-2.86	-3.21	-1.67	-3.39	1.38	0.18	-17.27
1978	-7.37	-3.61	2.06	10.55	0.39	-2.57	5.29	1.68	-1.25	-8.47	0.82	0.75	-3.15
1979	4.25	-3.62	6.60	-0.85	-3.81	2.40	0.52	4.87	-1.01	-7.16	0.82	1.98	4.19
1980	4.44	-1.46	-8.96	3.98	4.14	2.00	7.77	-0.29	-0.02	-0.85	7.44	-2.95	14.94
1981	-1.73	2.88	3.01	-0.61	-0.60	-1.50	-2.52	-7.43	-3.57	0.31	4.27	-1.57	-9.23
1982	-0.45	-5.36	-0.19	3.11	-3.41	-0.93	-0.41	11.46	-0.55	10.64	4.80	0.69	19.60
1983	2.79	3.43	1.56	8.51	-2.14	1.83	-1.87	1.42	1.39	-0.64	4.15	-1.36	20.27
1984	-3.02	-5.41	0.89	0.51	-5.63	2.49	-1.51	9.78	-1.45	0.06	-1.53	1.91	-3.73

	Jan	Feb	Mar	Apr	May	Jun	Jul	Aug	Sep	Oct	Nov	Dec	Year
1985	6.21	-0.22	-1.34	-0.69	4.55	1.53	0.90	-1.00	-0.40	3.44	7.12	5.07	27.66
1986	1.57	8.79	6.41	-1.90	5.20	0.85	-6.20	6.93	-6.89	6.23	1.94	-0.95	22.58
1987	13.82	3.06	3.63	-0.79	0.23	5.54	6.35	3.53	-2.50	-23.22	-8.02	5.74	2.26
1988	1.00	5.79	-4.03	2.22	-0.06	5.45	-0.61	-4.56	4.00	1.69	-1.59	2.56	11.85
1989	8.01	-3.58	1.56	5.46	2.54	-1.62	9.04	2.88	-1.63	-1.77	2.31	1.73	26.96
1990	-5.91	1.42	3.04	-1.86	8.28	0.14	0.85	-10.01	-6.19	-0.42	4.81	2.89	-4.34
1991	3.90	5.33	1.10	-0.89	4.83	-3.99	4.06	0.62	-0.88	1.73	-5.68	9.47	20.32
1992	1.72	1.37	-0.99	3.82	1.13	-2.31	2.27	-4.02	0.44	-1.39	2.45	-0.12	4.18
1993	0.27	1.84	1.91	-0.22	2.91	-0.32	0.67	3.16	-2.63	3.53	0.09	1.90	13.72
1994	5.97	-3.68	-5.11	1.26	2.08	-3.55	3.85	3.96	-1.79	1.69	-4.32	2.55	2.14
1995	0.25	4.35	3.65	3.93	3.33	2.04	3.34	-2.08	3.87	-0.70	6.71	0.84	33.45
1996	5.44	1.67	1.85	-0.32	1.33	0.20	-2.22	1.58	4.74	2.50	8.16	-1.13	26.01
1997	5.66	0.95	-4.28	6.46	4.59	4.66	7.17	-7.30	4.24	-6.33	5.12	1.09	22.64
1998	-0.02	8.08	2.97	3.00	-1.80	0.58	-0.77	-15.13	4.03	9.56	6.10	0.71	16.10
1999	1.93	-0.56	5.15	10.25	-2.13	3.89	-2.88	1.63	-4.55	3.80	1.38	5.29	24.74

Appendix G: About Financial Planning

This appendix is directed towards providing more information about Financial Planning.

What is Financial Planning?

Financial planning is the process of meeting your life goals through the proper management of your finances. Life goals can include buying a home, saving for your child's education or planning for retirement. It is a process that consists of specific steps that help you take a big-picture look at where you are financially. Using these steps, you can work out where you are now, what you may need in the future and what you must do to reach your goals.

This process involves gathering relevant financial information, setting life goals, examining your current financial status and coming up with a strategy or plan for how you can meet your goals given your current situation and future plans.

In the end, financial planning should provide direction and meaning to all your financial decisions, like how buying a particular investment product might help you pay off your mortgage faster or delay your retirement. By viewing each financial decision as part of a whole, you can consider its short and long-term effects on your life goals. You can also adapt more easily to life changes and feel more secure that your goals are on track.

How do I know if I need the advice of a Professional Financial Planner?

A good rule of thumb is: when in doubt, ask the expert.

You might want to consult a financial planner when you are doubtful that you have enough expertise to evaluate the level of risk in your investment portfolio or to adjust your retirement plan to reflect changing family circumstances.

If you have an immediate need or unexpected life event such as a birth, inheritance or major illness, you may not know how to make the financial adjustment, what is available to you and how you can cope.

Perhaps you want a second expert opinion about the financial plan you developed or are managing for yourself -- for peace of mind. Or you know you need to improve your current financial situation, but you don't know where to start.

Even in the absence of any doubts about your financial planning expertise, you might not feel you have the time to devote to it.

All these are good reasons to consult a financial planner.

How do I know if my Financial Planner is qualified to help me?

The FPSC is the standard-setting and licensing not-for-profit organization that licenses individuals who meet rigorous qualifications in experience, education, examination and ethics to earn the professional designation of Certified Financial Planners or CFP.

Finding the CFP trademark logo or letters or the words Certified Financial Planner, beside the name of a financial planning practitioner, will ensure that you have identified a professional who has been educated in, examined for, and has experience in all aspects of financial planning. You will know that you have found someone who has agreed to adhere to a strict code of professional conduct known as the CFP Code of Ethics. Additionally, you will know that the planner has made a life-long commitment to continuing education (30 hours per year) to keep their technical skills and theoretical knowledge current. There are currently 12,000 CFP practitioners in Canada and over 55,000 in 13 countries around the world. CFP is the mark of the professional financial planner.

To learn more about financial planning, how to find a financial planner nearest you, and about the CFP designation, visit www.cfp-ca.org.

Reproduced with the permission of Financial Planners Standards Council.

Appendix H: Weekday Gains By Decade

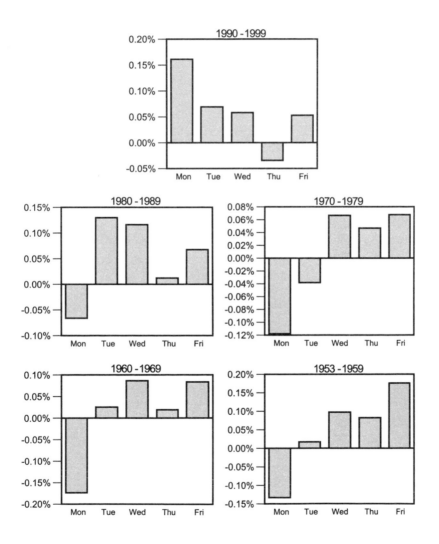

Appendix I: Super Seven Daily Gain by Decade 1950-1999

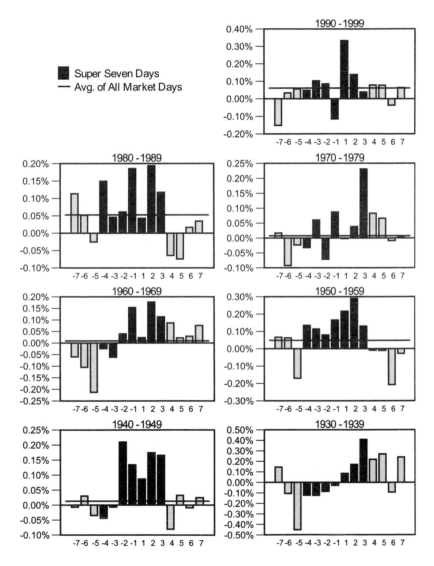

Appendix J: Super Seven Daily Gain by Month 1950-1999

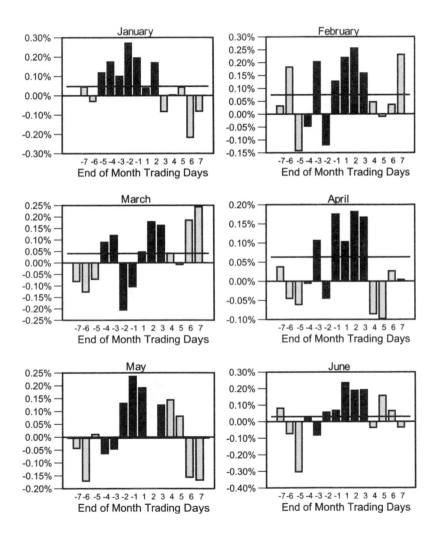

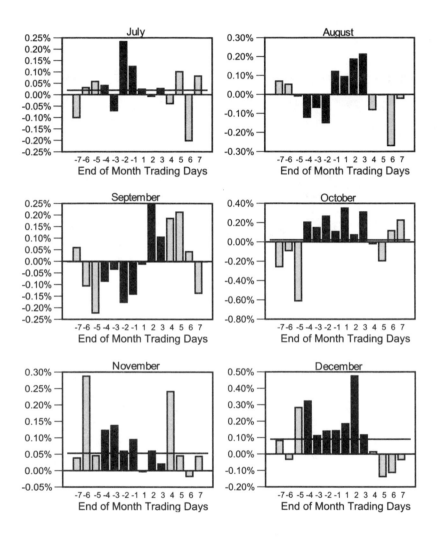

Appendix K: Super Seven versus Buy and Hold Dow Jones Yearly Results

How to Read the Table

Market % Increase = Yearly returns of the Dow

Super Seven % Increase = Yearly returns using the Super Seven strategy for every month of the year

Year	Super Seven % Increase	Market % Increase
1950	7.48	17.64
1951	24.50	14.36
1952	11.07	8.43
1953	4.02	-3.77
1954	23.34	43.97
1955	13.04	20.77
1956	21.20	2.27
1957	7.07	-12.77
1958	19.39	33.97
1959	13.50	16.40
1960	-0.87	-9.35
1961	23.76	18.70
1962	9.80	-10.81
1963	7.96	17.01
1964	4.75	14.56
1965	12.73	10.89
1966	-13.54	-18.94
1967	2.85	15.20
1968	7.07	4.28
1969	-0.80	-15.19
1970	20.47	4.81
1971	8.98	6.12
1972	13.48	14.58

Year	Super Seven % Increase	Market % Increase
1973	-5.05	-16.58
1974	-12.52	-27.58
1975	15.48	38.33
1976	3.98	17.87
1977	-8.17	-17.27
1978	7.51	-3.15
1979	-3.21	4.19
1980	1.09	14.94
1981	6.38	-9.23
1982	3.98	19.60
1983	3.73	20.27
1984	9.42	-3.73
1985	6.66	27.66
1986	6.94	22.58
1987	18.58	2.26
1988	24.44	11.85
1989	13.58	26.96
1990	14.14	-4.34
1991	14.53	20.32
1992	5.20	4.18
1993	3.15	13.72
1994	4.64	2.14
1995	14.48	33.45
1996	6.46	26.01
1997	19.08	22.64
1998	-13.70	16.10
1999	15.61	24.74
Compound Growth*	4,452	5,624
Yearly Average Growth**	7.94	8.43

* Total Growth (2nd last row of table) = total compounded growth over fifty years

** Yearly Average Growth (last row of the table) = Yearly Average (geometric) growth rate over fifty years

Appendix L: Super Seven Statistics

Super Seven Statistics, 1950 to 1999

	-7	-6	-5	-4	-3	-2	-1	1	2	3	4	5	6	7	Only Super Seven Days	Market Days 1950-1999
Daily Average Percent	-0.0031	-0.0099	-0.075	0.055	0.052	0.039	0.096	0.123	0.167	0.126	0.035	0.016	-0.042	0.030	0.094	0.0355%
Daily t-stat	-1.15	-1.39	-2.77	0.58	0.46	0.08	**1.72**	**2.38**	**3.99**	**2.55**	-0.03	-0.57	-2.39	-0.18	**4.43**	N/A
Frequency Percent	50.67	47.83	49.00	55.33	54.17	53.83	55.33	57.83	60.67	56.00	55.00	50.33	49.50	51.67	56.17	52.99%

t-statistic for the hypothesis that the average daily returns are greater than the overall daily average of the market at the 5% level are bolded. At this level, the values are considered to be statistically significant

Appendix M: Fantastic Five Statistics

Fantastic Five Statistics, 1953 to 1999

	1	2	3	4	5	Fantastic Five	Market Days 1950-1999
Daily Average	0.10%	0.05%	0.03%	0.08%	0.06%	0.06%	0.04%
Daily t-tat	**1.784814413**	0.48465001	-0.039423317	1.424345772	0.591754958	**1.905918353**	N/A
Daily Frequency	58.00%	53.17%	50.17%	58.33%	54.50%	54.83%	52.99%

t-statistic for the hypothesis that the average daily returns are greater than the overall daily average of the market at the 5% level are bolded.

Appendix N: Fantastic Five Daily Gain by Decade 1950-1999

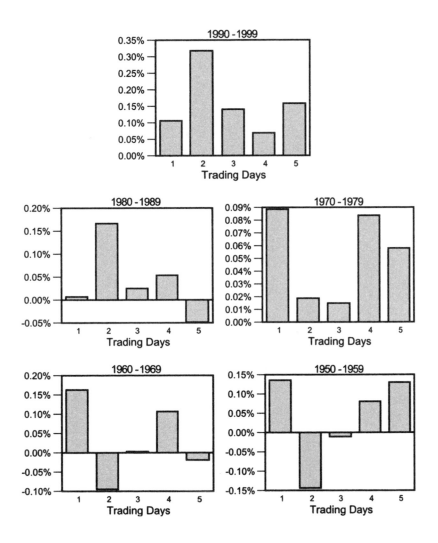

Appendix O: Fantastic Five Daily Gain by Month 1953-1999

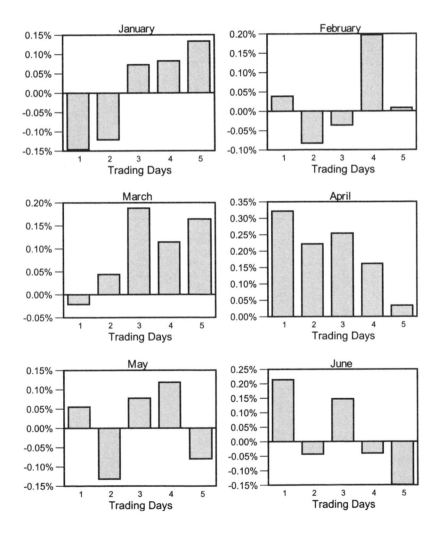

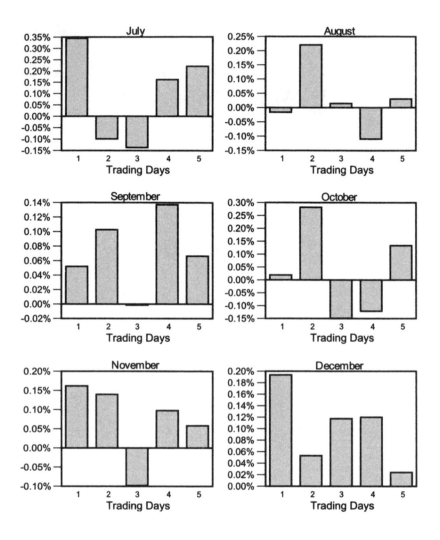

Appendix P: Witches' Hangover Daily Gain by Decade

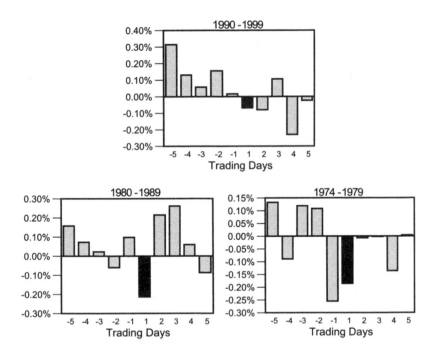

Appendix Q: 100-Day and 55-Day Cycles by Decade

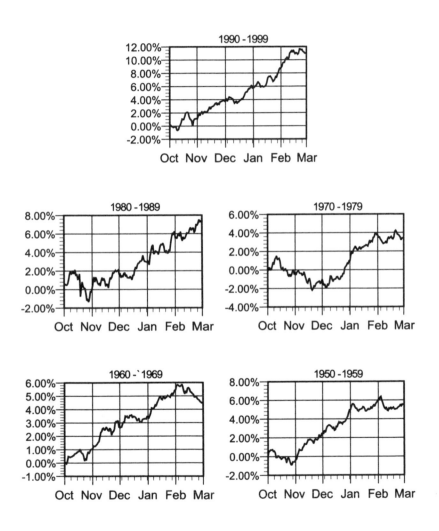

Appendix R: Various Index Shares

The following lists outline the different types of index shares available for trading on the Amex stock market, with their corresponding trade symbols.

Index Shares on Broad-Based Indexes

- Nasdaq-100 Index Tracking StockSM -- based on the Nasdaq-100 Index® (QQQ)
- SPDRs® -- based on the Standard & Poor's 500 Composite Stock Price Index® (SPY)
- MidCap SPDRsTM -- based on the S&P500 MidCap 400 IndexTM (MDY)
- DIAMONDS® -- based on the Dow Jones Industrial AverageSM (DIA)
- iShares Dow Jones U.S. Total Market Index FundTM -- based on Dow Jones U.S. Total Market IndexTM (IYY)
- iShares S&P/TSE 60 Index FundTM -- based on the S&P/TSE 60 IndexTM (IKC)
- iShares S&P 500 Index FundTM -- based on the S&P 500 IndexTM (IVV)
- iShares S&P 500/BARRA Growth Index FundTM based on the S&P 500 IndexTM (IVW)
- iShares S&P 500/BARRA Value Index FundTM based on the S&P 500 IndexTM (IVE)
- iShares S&P MidCap 400 Index FundTM, based on the S&P MidCap 400IndexTM (IJH)
- iShares S&P SmallCap 600 Index FundTM based on the S&P SmallCap 600IndexTM (IJR)
- iShares Russell 1000 Index FundTM -- based on the Russell 1000 IndexTM (IWB)

- iShares Russell 1000 Growth Index FundTM -- based on the Russell 1000IndexTM (IWF)
- iShares Russell 1000 Value Index FundTM -- based on the Russell 1000 IndexTM (IWD)
- iShares Russell 2000 Index FundTM -- based on the Russell 2000 IndexTM (IWM)
- iShares Russell 3000 Index FundTM -- based on the Russell 3000 IndexTM (IWV)

Index Shares on International Indexes

- iShares MSCI Australia Index Fund (EWA)
- iShares MSCI Austria Index Fund (EWO)
- iShares MSCI Belgium Index Fund (EWK)
- iShares MSCI Brazil Index Fund (EWZ)
- iShares MSCI Canada Index Fund (EWC)
- iShares MSCI France Index Fund (EWQ)
- iShares MSCI Germany Index Fund (EWG)
- iShares MSCI Hong Kong Index Fund (EWH)
- iShares MSCI Italy Index Fund (EWI)
- iShares MSCI Japan Index Fund (EWJ)
- iShares MSCI Malaysia Index Fund (EWM)
- iShares MSCI Mexico Index Fund (EWW)
- iShares MSCI Netherlands Index Fund (EWN)
- iShares MSCI Singapore Index Fund (EWS)
- iShares MSCI South Korea Index Fund (EWY)
- iShares MSCI Spain Index Fund (EWP)
- iShares MSCI Sweden Index Fund (EWD)
- iShares MSCI Switzerland Index Fund (EWL)
- iShares MSCI Taiwan Index Fund (EWT)
- iShares MSCI United Kingdom Index Fund (EWU)

Index Shares on Sector Indexes

- Select Sector SPDR - The Basic Industries Fund (XLB)
- Select Sector SPDR - The Consumer Services Select Fund (XLV)
- Select Sector SPDR - Consumer Staples Select Fund (XLP)
- Select Sector SPDR - Cyclical/Transportation Fund (XLY)
- Select Sector SPDR - The Energy Fund (XLE)
- Select Sector SPDR - The Financial Fund (XLF)

- Select Sector SPDR - The Industrial Fund (XLI)
- Select Sector SPDR - The Technology Fund (XLK)
- Select Sector SPDR - The Utilities Fund (XLU)
- iShares Dow Jones U.S. Basic Materials Sector Index Fund (IYM)
- iShares Dow Jones U.S. Chemicals Index Fund (IYD)
- iShares Dow Jones U.S. Consumer Cyclical Sector Index Fund (IYC)
- iShares Dow Jones U.S. Consumer Non-Cyclical Sector Index Fund (IYK)
- iShares Dow Jones U.S. Energy Sector Index Fund (IYE)
- iShares Dow Jones U.S. Financial Sector Index Fund (IYF)
- iShares Dow Jones U.S. Financial Services Sector Index Fund (IYG)
- iShares Dow Jones U.S. Healthcare Sector Index Fund (IYH)
- iShares Dow Jones U.S. Industrial Sector Index Fund (IYJ)
- iShares Dow Jones U.S. Internet Index Fund (IYV)
- iShares Dow Jones U.S. Real Estate Sector Index Fund (IYR)
- iShares Dow Jones U.S. Technology Sector Index Fund (IYW)
- iShares Dow Jones U.S. Telecommunications Sector Index Fund (IYZ)
- iShares Dow Jones U.S. Utilities Sector Index Fund (IDU)

Bibliography

1. Alexander, Colin. <u>Streetsmart Guide to Timing the Stock Market</u>. New York: McGraw-Hill, 1999.

2. Ariel, Robert A. "A Monthly Effect in Stock Returns." <u>Journal of Financial Economics</u>. 18 (1990): 161-174.

3. Ariel, Robert A. "High Stock Returns Before Holidays: Existence and Evidence on Possible Causes." <u>Journal of Finance</u>. 45 (1987): 1611-1626.

4. Cadsby, Ted. <u>The Power of Index Funds</u>. Toronto: Stoddart, 1999.

5. Cross, F. "The Behavior of Stock Prices on Fridays and Mondays." <u>Financial Analysts Journal</u>. November-December (1973): 67-69.

6. Gardner, David, and Tom Gardner, eds. <u>The Motley Fool Investment Guide</u>. New York: Simon & Schuster, 1996.

7. Gonzales, Michael. "Buying Stocks? Consider the Turn-of-the Month Effect." <u>Wall Street Journal</u>. 7 November 1995, late ed: C1-C2.

8. Harding, Sy. <u>Riding the Bear</u>. Massachusetts: Adams Media Corporation, 1999.

9. Hirsch, Yale. <u>1998 Stock Trader's Almanac</u>. New Jersey: The Hirsch Organization Inc.,1997.

10. Lynch, Peter. <u>One Up on Wall Street</u>. New York: Simon & Schuster, 1989.

11. McLean, Bethany. "Best Mutual Funds: The Skeptic's Guide to Mutual Funds." <u>Fortune Investor</u> 15 March 1999 <http://www.fortune.com/fortune/investor/1999/03/15/way.html>.

12. O'Higgins, Michael. <u>Beating the Dow</u>. New York: HarperPerenial, 1992.

13. O'Neil, William J. <u>How To Make Money in Stocks, Second Edition</u>. New York: McGraw-Hill, 1995.

14. Pettengill, Glenn N. "Holiday Closings and Security Returns." <u>Journal of Financial Research</u>. 12 (1989): 57-67.

INDEX